NIKON COOLPIX P950 USER GUIDE

The Ultimate Handbook for Mastering the Functionalities and Features of this Digital Camera

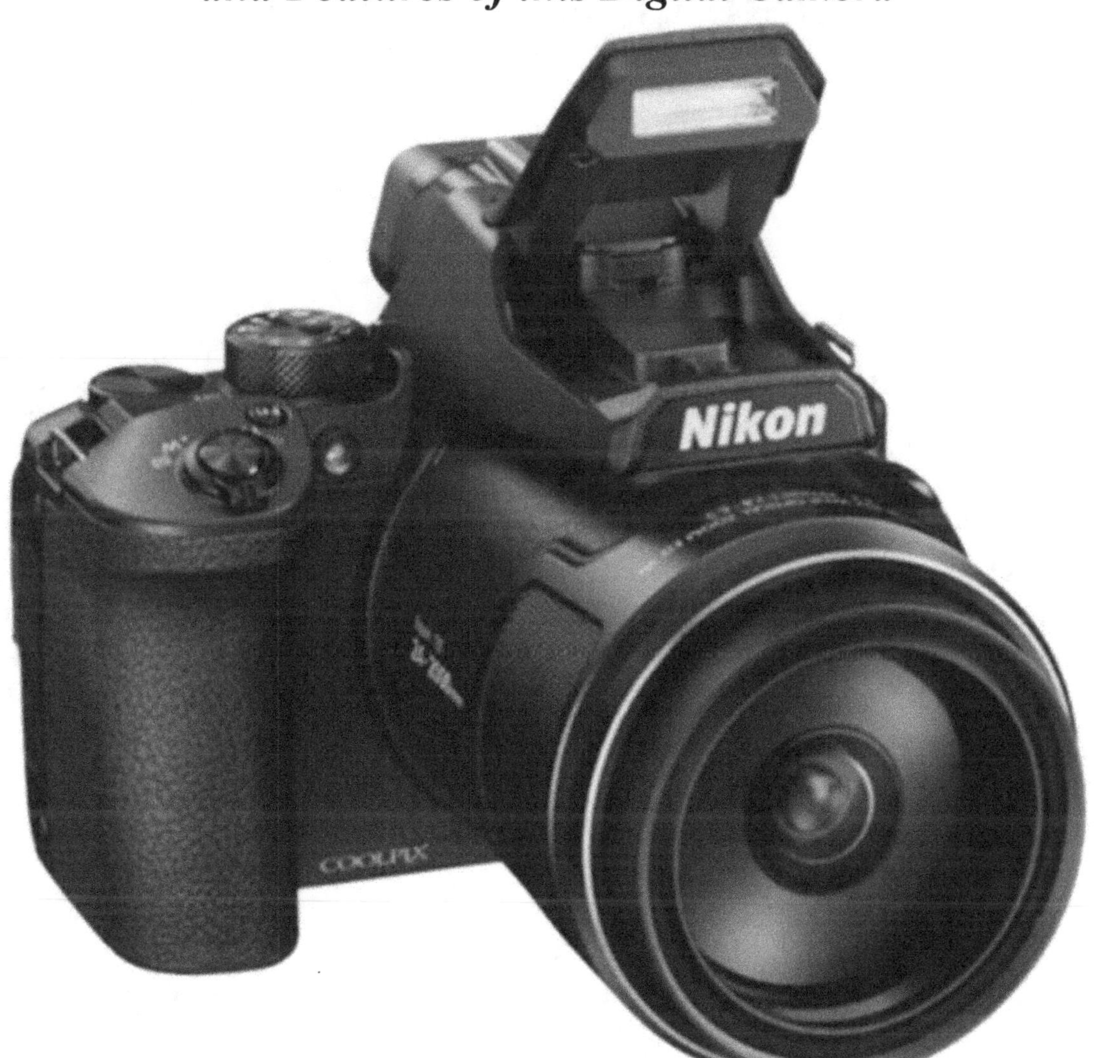

JAMES D. SALA

Copyright © 2024 James D. Sala

All rights reserved.

No part of this publication may be reproduced, distributed, or transmitted in any form or by any means, including photocopying, recording, or other electronic or mechanical methods, without the prior written permission of the publisher, except in the case of brief quotations embodied in critical reviews and certain other non-commercial uses permitted by copyright law

TABLE OF CONTENTS

DISCLAIMER 4
CHAPTER ONE 6
INTRODUCTION 6
Overview of Nikon Coolpix P950 6
Features Overview 7
What's in the Box 9
CHAPTER TWO 16
GETTING STARTED 16
Camera Parts and Controls 16
Turning the Camera On and Off 23
Setting the Date and Time 24
The Menu System 26
CHAPTER THREE 30
SHOOTING MODES 30
Auto Mode 30
Scene Modes 32
P, S, A, and M Modes (Program, Shutter Priority, Aperture Priority, Manual) 34
Movie Mode 37
CHAPTER FOUR 40
TAKING PICTURES 40
Using the Zoom Lens 40
Focusing 41
Exposure Basics (Aperture, Shutter Speed, ISO) 43
White Balance 45
Metering Modes 46
Using the Flash 47
Reviewing Images 49
CHAPTER FIVE 52
PLAYBACK AND EDITING 52

Playing Back Images 52
Deleting Images 53
In-Camera Editing 55
CHAPTER SIX 58
ADVANCED FEATURES 58
Using the Electronic Viewfinder (EVF) 58
Wi-Fi and Bluetooth Connectivity 60
Shooting in RAW format 61
Customizing Buttons and Menus 63
CHAPTER SEVEN 66
ACCESSSORIES 66
Tripods 66
External Flashes 70
Remote Controls 71
Carrying Cases 74
CHAPTER EIGHT 78
TROUBLESHOOTING 78
Common Camera Problems 78
Error Messages 79
Cleaning and Maintenance Tips 81
Firmware Updates 82
CHAPTER NINE 86
APPENDIX 86
Specifications 86
Additional Notes 87
Warranty Information 87
Glossary of Terms 88
Contacting Nikon Support 90

DISCLAIMER

The contents of this book are provided for informational and entertainment purposes only. The author and publisher make no representations or warranties with respect to the accuracy, applicability, completeness, or suitability of the contents of this book for any purpose.

The information contained within this book is based on the author's personal experiences, research, and opinions, and it is not intended to substitute for professional advice. Readers are encouraged to consult appropriate professionals in the field regarding their individual situations and circumstances.

The author and publisher shall not be liable for any loss, injury, or damage allegedly arising from any information or suggestions contained within this book. Any reliance you place on such information is strictly at your own risk.

Furthermore, the inclusion of any third-party resources, websites, or references does not imply endorsement or responsibility for the content or services provided by these entities.

Readers are encouraged to use their own discretion and judgment in applying any information or recommendations contained within this book to their own lives and situations.

All rights reserved. No part of this book may be reproduced, distributed, or transmitted in any form or by any means, including photocopying, recording, or other electronic or mechanical methods, without the prior written permission of the publisher, except in the case of brief quotations embodied in critical reviews and certain other non-commercial uses permitted by copyright law.

Thank you for reading and understanding this disclaimer

CHAPTER ONE
INTRODUCTION

Overview of Nikon Coolpix P950

The Nikon Coolpix P950 is a bridge camera known for its **astounding 83x optical zoom lens**, bringing faraway subjects incredibly close. It's ideal for photographers who want to capture detailed images of:

- Wildlife
- Birds
- Landscapes
- Aircraft
- Even celestial objects like the moon

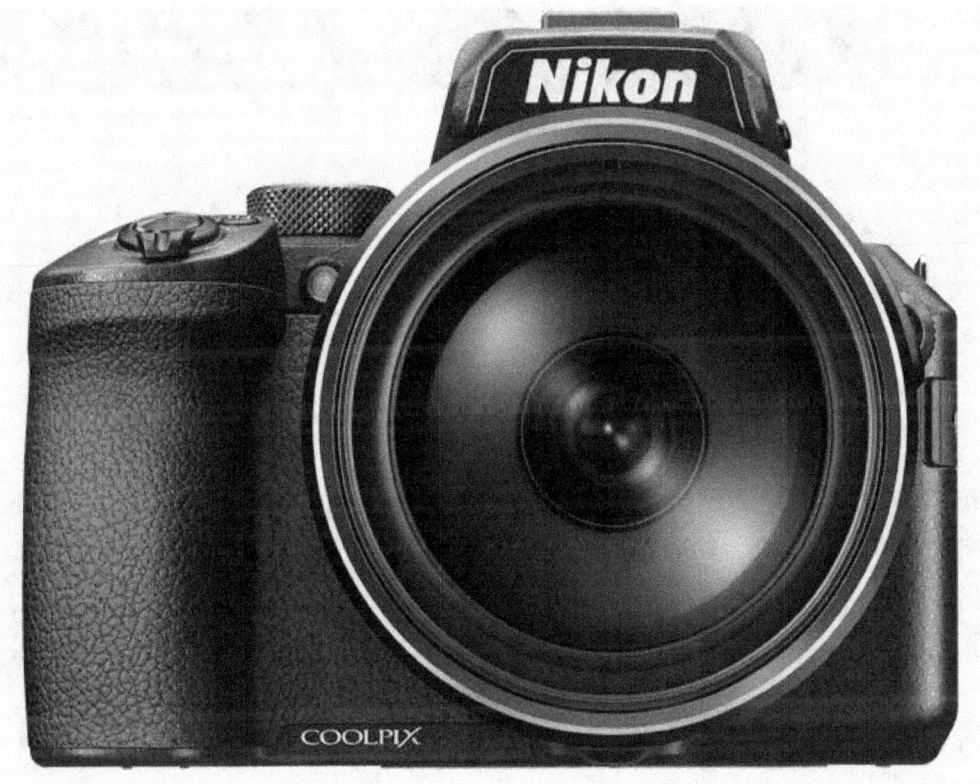

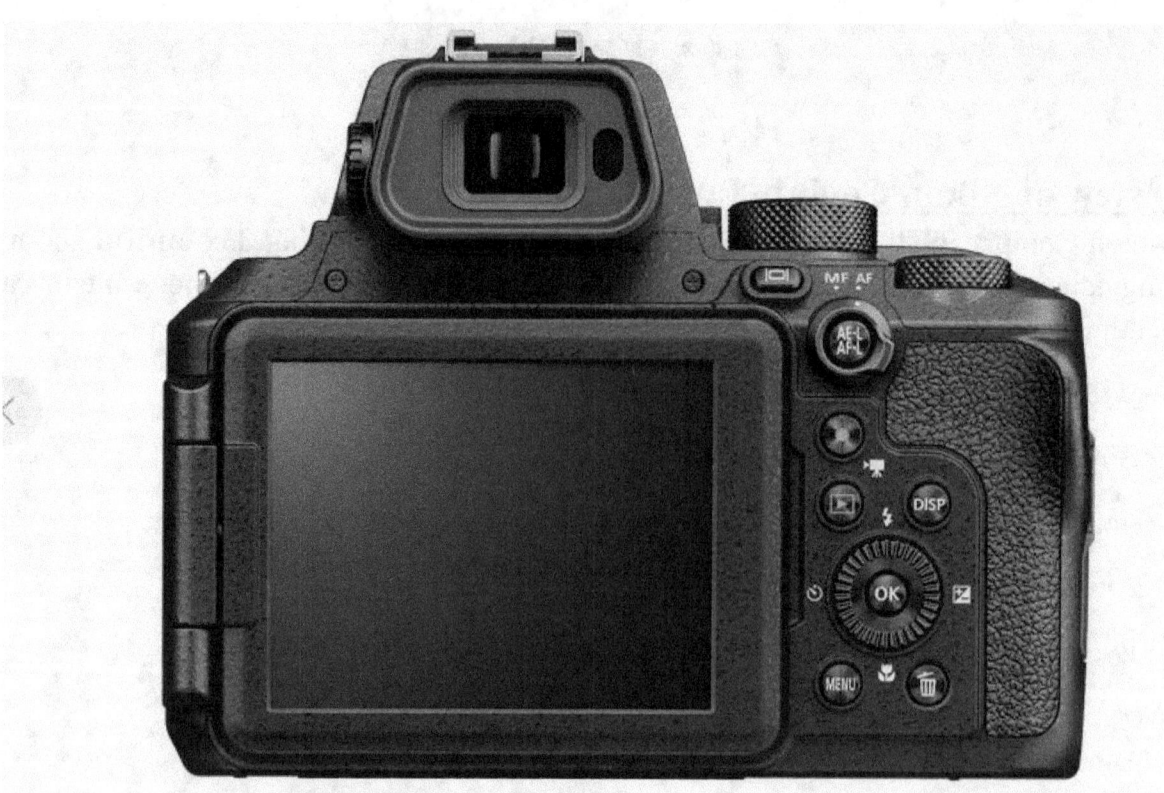

Things to Consider:

- **Image Quality:** While the zoom is impressive, low-light image quality might not be ideal for everyone.

- **Size and Weight:** The P950 is a bigger camera compared to point-and-shoots, but lighter than DSLRs.

- **Zoom and Stability:** A tripod is highly recommended for sharp photos at high zoom ranges due to potential camera shake.

The Nikon Coolpix P950 is a compelling option for photographers who prioritize capturing distant subjects in detail. Its exceptional zoom range and user-friendly features make it a great choice for wildlife, nature, and travel enthusiasts.

Features Overview

The Nikon Coolpix P950 bridges the gap between point-and-shoots and DSLRs, boasting impressive features ideal for capturing the distant world. Here's a breakdown of its key functionalities:

Megazoom Lens:

- Be the star of wildlife and birding photography with the headline feature - a staggering 83x optical zoom NIKKOR lens.
- This translates to a focal range of 24mm (wide) to a mind-blowing 2000mm (telephoto), bringing faraway subjects right into your frame.
- And with Dynamic Fine Zoom, you can achieve an even crazier 4000mm zoom digitally (be aware of potential quality loss at such high digital zoom).

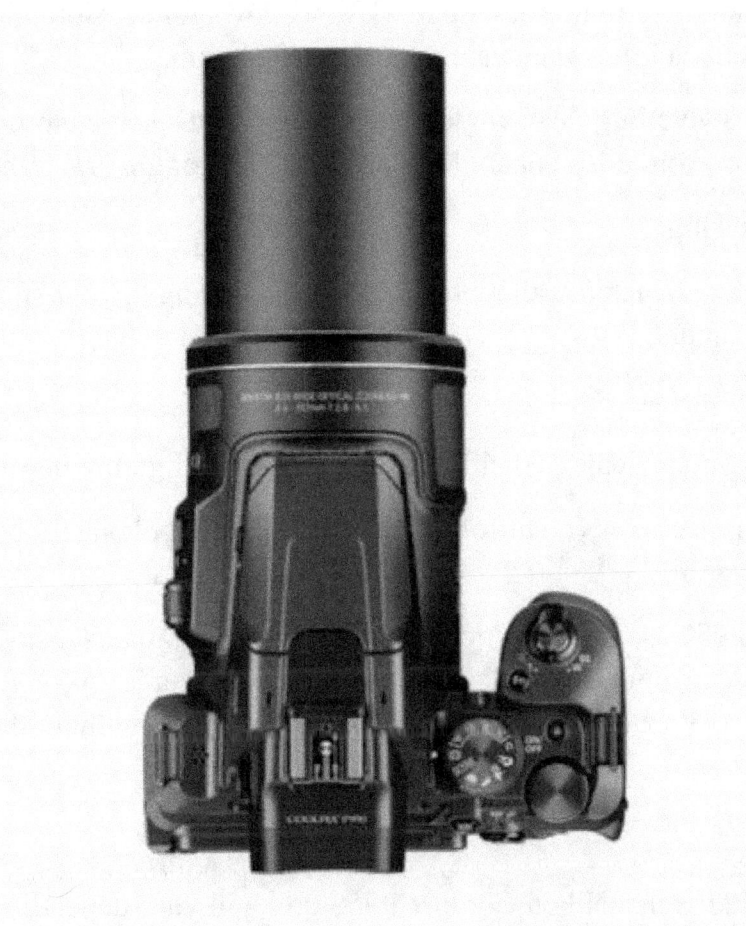

Image Quality:

- A 16-megapixel CMOS sensor captures good quality images in well-lit situations.
- Low-light performance might be limited due to the smaller sensor size compared to larger cameras.

Shooting Modes:

- Auto mode takes care of settings for beginners.

- Scene modes offer presets for specific situations like landscapes, portraits, or night scenes.
- Unleash your creativity with manual shooting modes (P, S, A, and M) that provide complete control over aperture, shutter speed, and ISO.
- The P950 also shoots up to 4K UHD video for capturing smooth, high-resolution footage.

Viewing and Composition:

- A high-resolution Electronic Viewfinder (EVF) allows for comfortable framing and image review, especially helpful when using the powerful zoom.
- A tilting and swivelling Vari-angle touchscreen LCD screen provides flexibility for composing shots from different angles, perfect for low-angle or overhead shots.

Connectivity and Sharing:

- Built-in Wi-Fi and Bluetooth allow for easy image sharing to your smartphone and remote control of the camera.

Additional Features:

- A hot shoe lets you attach external flashes for improved lighting in low-light situations.
- A microphone jack allows you to connect an external microphone for better audio recording during video capture.

The Nikon Coolpix P950 is a feature-rich option for photographers who prioritize capturing distant subjects with exceptional detail. Its user-friendly features make it a great choice for wildlife, nature, and travel enthusiasts who want a powerful zoom without the bulk of a DSLR.

What's in the Box

The typical items included in a Nikon Coolpix P950 box will vary depending on the retailer and whether you purchase a bundle with additional accessories. However, the standard inclusions should be:

- **Nikon COOLPIX P950 Digital Camera:** The star of the show, the P950 camera itself.

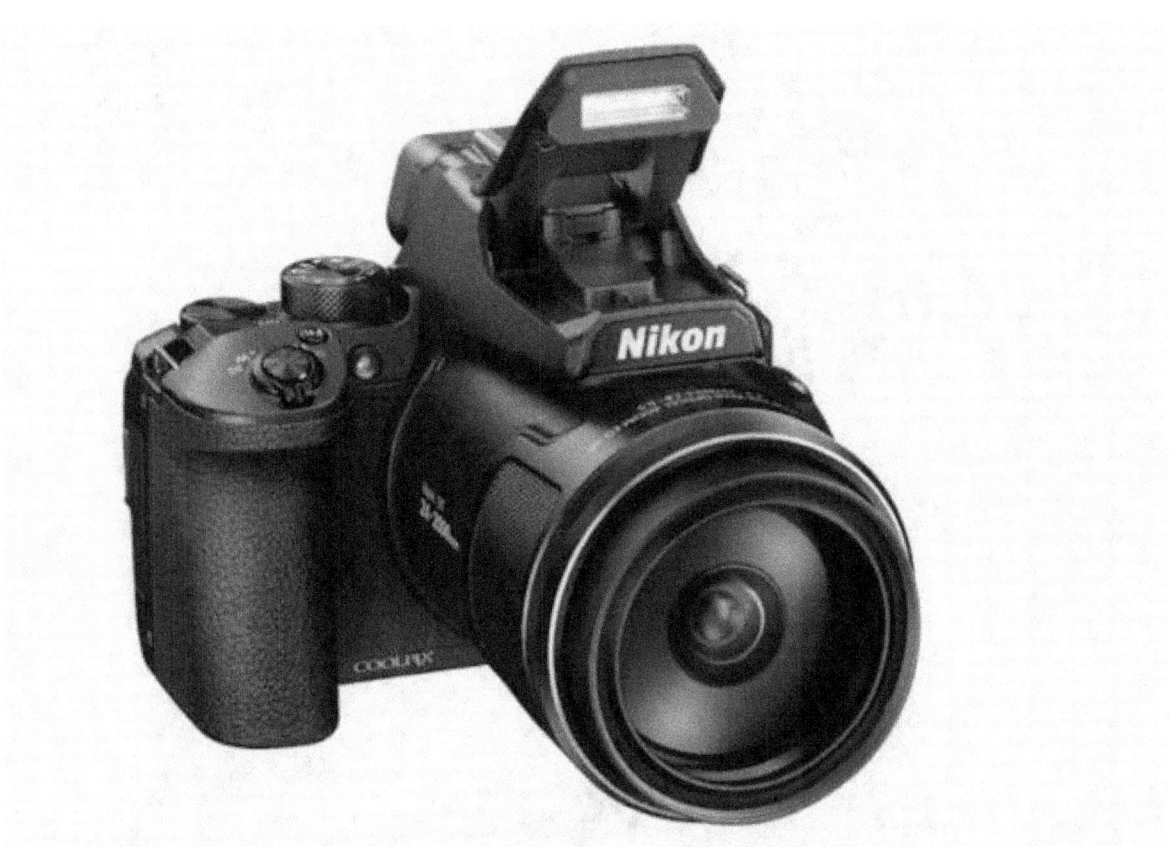

- **Nikon EN-EL20a Rechargeable Lithium-Ion Battery Pack:** This provides power for your camera.

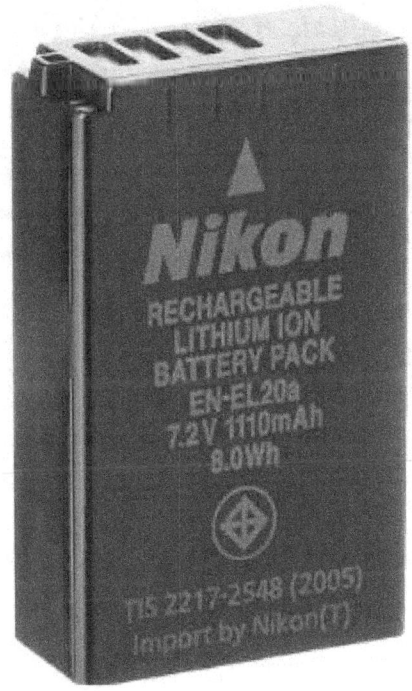

- **Nikon EH-73P Charging AC Adapter:** This recharges your EN-EL20a battery.

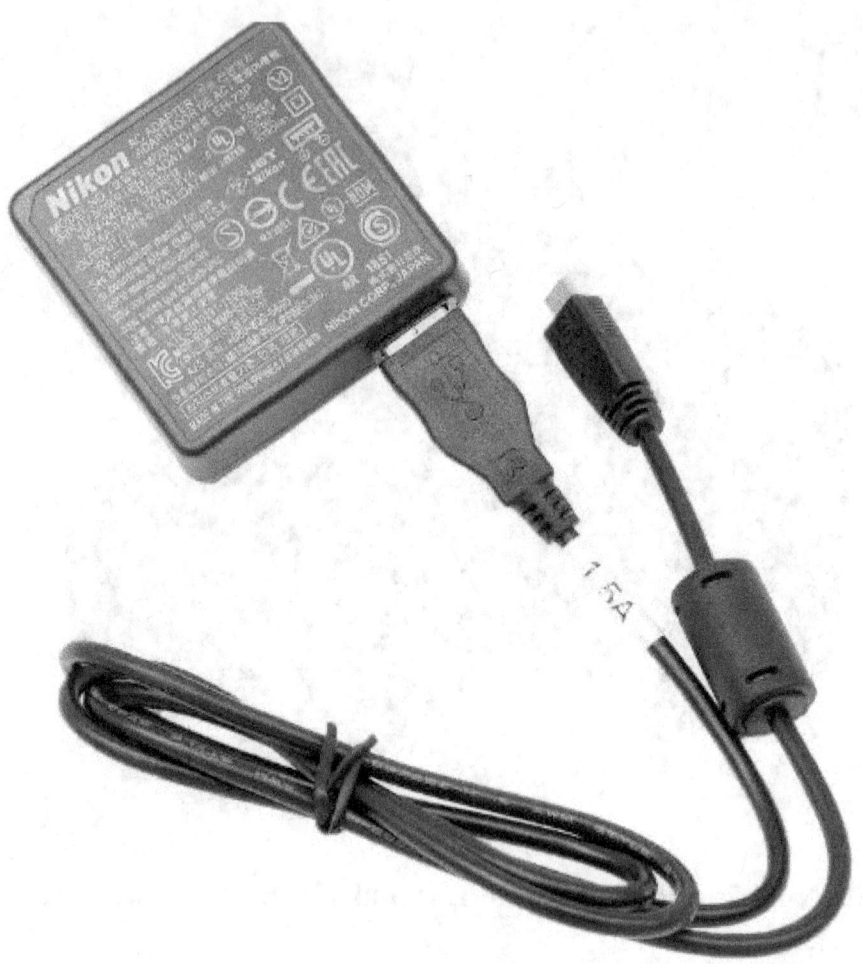

- **Nikon UC-E21 USB Type-A Male to Type-B Micro Male Cable (Black):** This cable allows you to connect your camera to your computer for transferring photos and charging the battery (with an optional AC adapter).

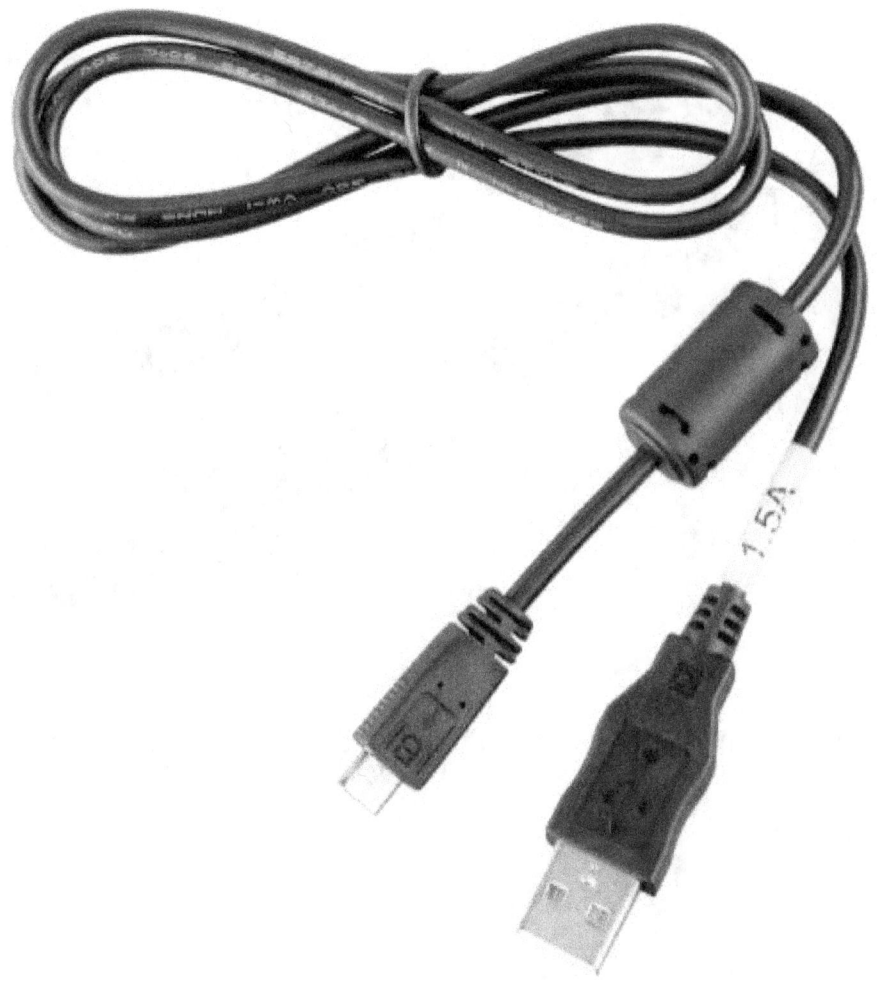

- **Nikon AN-DC3 Camera Strap (Black):** A comfortable strap to carry your camera around your neck or shoulder.

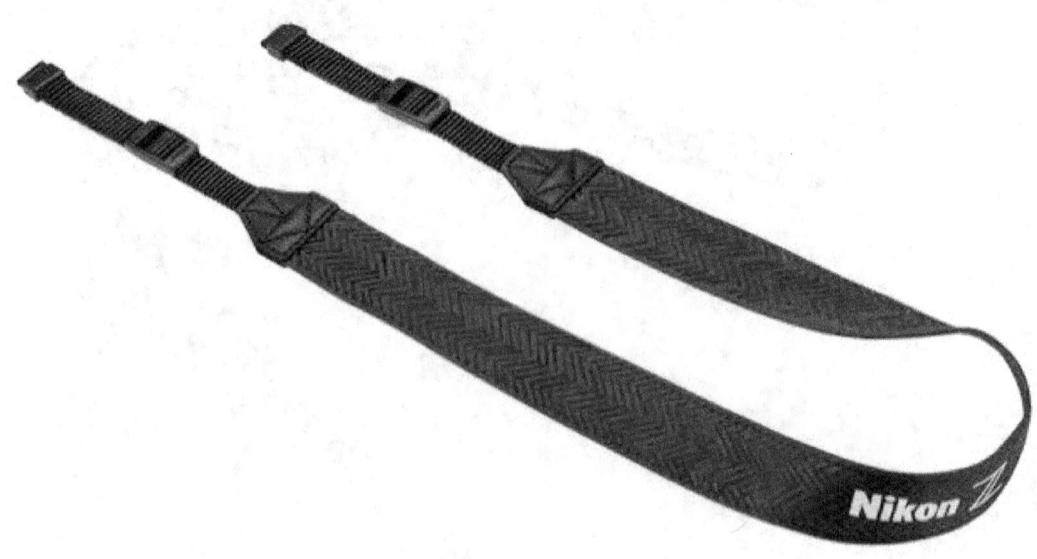

- **Nikon 67mm Snap-On Lens Cap:** Protects your valuable lens from dust and scratches.

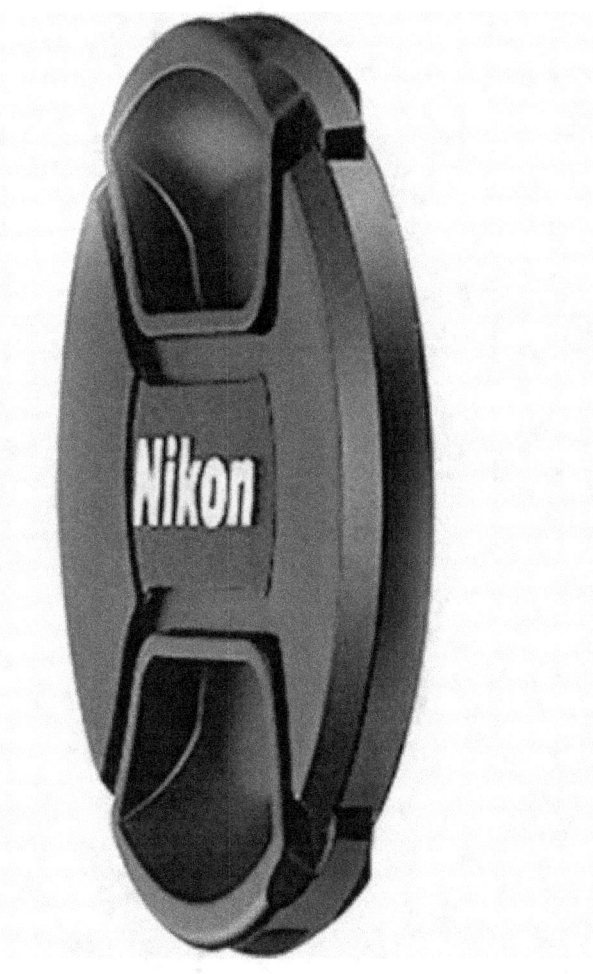

- **HN-CP20 Lens Hood:** This helps reduce lens flare and stray light for sharper images.

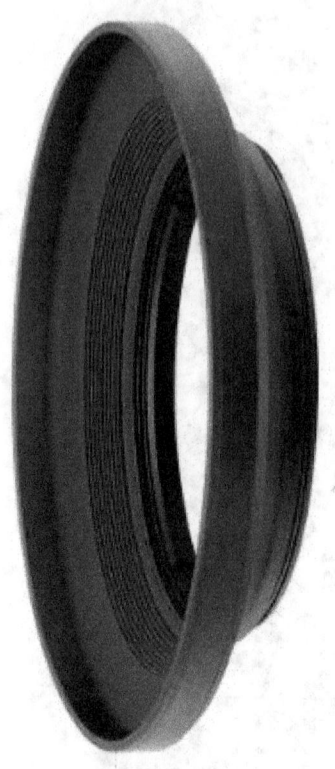

Optional Extras in Bundles:

- **Memory Card:** The P950 doesn't come with a memory card, so you'll need one to store your photos and videos.

- **Carrying Case:** A padded case protects your camera during transport.

- **External Flash:** Provides additional lighting for low-light situations.

- **Tripod:** Essential for sharp photos at high zoom ranges due to potential camera shake.

- **Software:** Some bundles might include photo editing or organizing software.

It's important to check the specific contents listed by the retailer before purchasing to ensure you're getting everything you need.

CHAPTER TWO
GETTING STARTED

Camera Parts and Controls

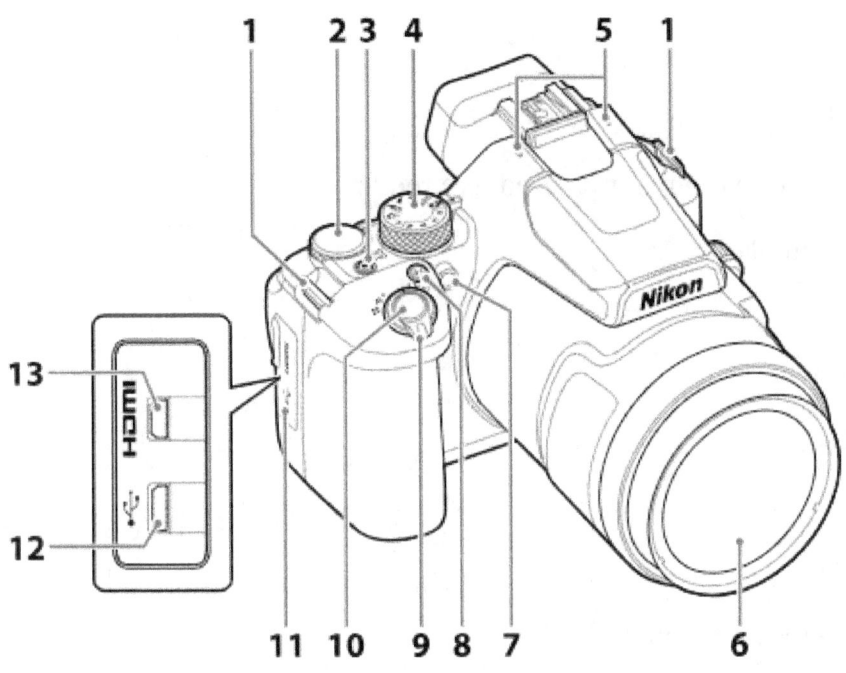

1. Eyelet for Strap

    - Attaching the strap

2. Command Dial

3. Power Switch/Power-on Lamp (Charge Lamp)

    - Power-on lamp (charge lamp)

    - Charging the battery

    - Camera setup

4. Mode Dial

    - Selecting a shooting mode

5. Microphone (Stereo)

- Basic operations of movie recording and playback
- Zoom microphone

6. Lens
7. Self-timer Lamp
    - Self-timer
    - Smile timer
    - Red-eye reduction lamp
    - [Auto with red-eye reduction] / [Red-eye reduction]
    - AF-assist illuminator
    - AF assist
8. Function Button
    - Using the function button
9. Zoom Control
    - : Wide-angle
        - Using the zoom control
    - : Telephoto
        - Using the zoom control
    - : Thumbnail playback
        - Thumbnail playback/calendar display
    - : Playback zoom
        - Playback zoom
10. Shutter-release Button
    - Shooting still images
    - The shutter-release button
11. Connector Cover
    - Charging the battery
    - Viewing images on a TV

- Transferring images to a computer

12. Micro-USB Connector
    - Charging the battery
    - Transferring images to a computer

13. HDMI Micro Connector (Type D)
    - Viewing images on a TV

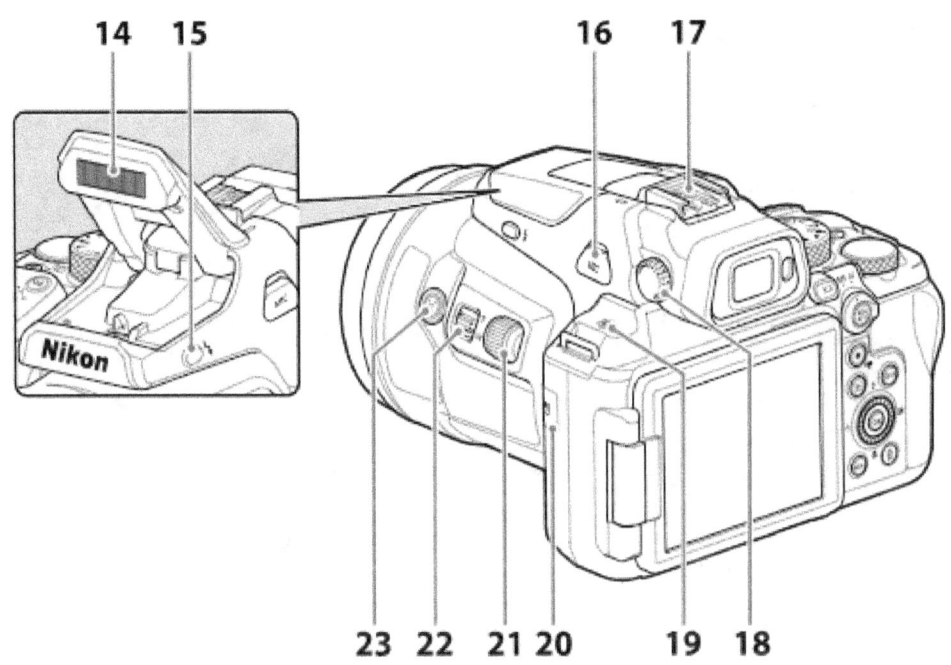

14. Built-in Flash
    - Using the built-in flash
    - Flash mode

15. Flash Pop-up Button
    - Using the built-in flash
    - Flash mode

16. External Microphone Connector Cover

- External microphone

17. Accessory Shoe
    - Accessory shoe cover
    - Speedlights (external flash units)

18. Diopter Adjustment Control
    - Diopter adjustment of the viewfinder

19. Speaker
    - Operations during movie playback
    - Sound settings

20. Accessory Terminal
    - Remote control accessories

21. Side Dial
    - Assigning functions to the side dial

22. Side Zoom Control
    - : Wide-angle
    - : Telephoto
    - Using the side zoom control

23. Snap-back Zoom Button
    - Using the snap-back zoom (temporarily widening the visible range)

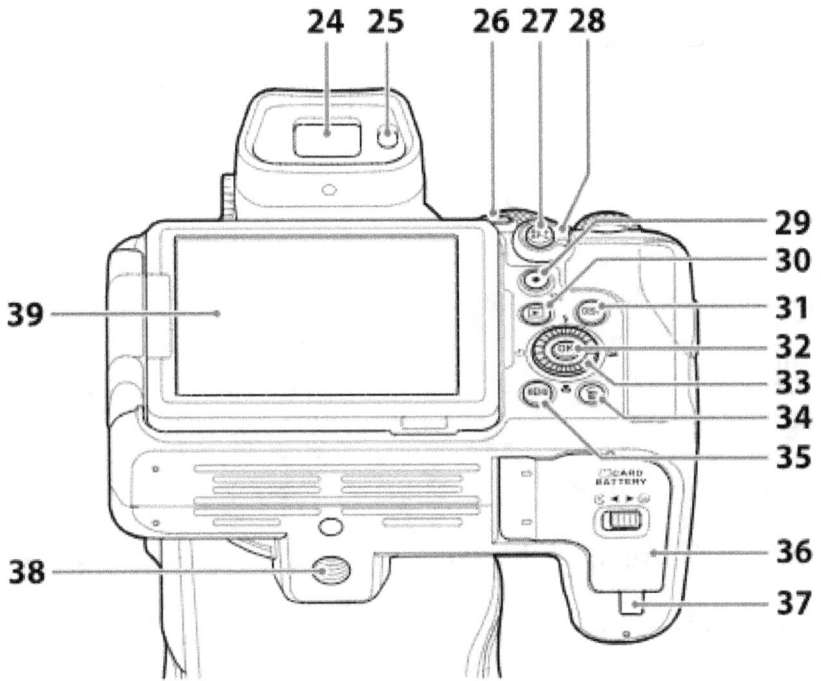

24. Electronic Viewfinder
    - Switching between the monitor and viewfinder
25. Eye Sensor
    - Switching between the monitor and viewfinder
26. Monitor Button
    - Switching between the monitor and viewfinder
27. AE-L/AF-L Button
    - Focus lock
    - AE/AF lock
28. Focus-mode Selector
    - Using autofocus
    - Using manual focus
29. Movie Record Button

- Recording movies
- Basic operations of movie recording and playback

30. Playback Button
    - Playing back images

31. Display Button
    - Switching the information displayed on the screen

32. Apply Selection Button
    - Menu operations

33. Rotary Multi Selector (Multi Selector)
    - Pressing up, down, left, or right on the multi selector is expressed as ▲, ▼, ◄, or ►.
    - Setting the flash mode, self-timer, focus mode, and exposure compensation
    - Menu operations

34. Delete Button
    - Deleting images

35. Menu Button
    - Menu operations
    - Menu lists

36. Battery-chamber/Memory Card Slot Cover
    - Inserting the battery and memory card

37. Power Connector Cover (for optional AC adapter)
    - AC adapter

38. Tripod Socket

39. Monitor
    - The monitor/viewfinder
    - Opening the monitor

2.2 Inserting the Battery and Memory Card

Here's a guide on inserting the battery and memory card into your Nikon Coolpix P950 with images:

Requirements:

- Nikon Coolpix P950 camera
- Nikon EN-EL20a rechargeable lithium-ion battery (or compatible replacement)
- SD, SDHC, or SDXC memory card (recommended speed Class 6 or faster for video recording)

Steps:

1. **Turn off the camera:** Ensure the camera is completely powered off before inserting the battery or memory card.

2. **Open the battery/memory card compartment cover:** Locate the compartment cover on the bottom of the camera. It's usually near the tripod mount. Slide the latch in the direction indicated by the arrow (usually to the right) and lift the cover to open it.

3. **Insert the battery:**

- Hold the battery with the positive (+) terminal facing up (as indicated by the marking on the battery compartment).
- Slide the battery into the compartment according to the battery compartment markings.
- Gently press down on the battery until it clicks into place.

4. **Insert the memory card:**

- Locate the memory card slot inside the compartment. It's usually next to the battery compartment.
- Hold the memory card with the label facing towards you and the gold contacts facing down.
- Slide the memory card into the slot until it clicks into place.

5. **Close the compartment cover:** Push the cover back down until it snaps shut.

Removing the Battery or Memory Card:

- Turn off the camera and ensure it's not in use.
- Open the battery/memory card compartment cover as described earlier.

- To remove the battery, gently press the orange battery latch located on the side of the compartment (opposite the contacts). The battery will pop up slightly, allowing you to remove it.
- To remove the memory card, gently push it into the slot until it clicks. Then, you can pull it out of the camera.

Important Notes:

- Always format the memory card in the camera before using it for the first time. Formatting erases any existing data on the card.
- Ensure the battery and memory card are inserted correctly according to the markings on the camera compartment. Forcing them in the wrong way can damage the camera or the card.
- It's recommended to use genuine Nikon batteries for optimal performance and lifespan.

By following these steps, you can easily insert the battery and memory card into your Nikon Coolpix P950 and start capturing stunning images.

Turning the Camera On and Off

Here's how to turn your Nikon Coolpix P950 on and off:

Turning On:

1. Locate the power button on the top right side of the camera, near the shutter release button. It's usually a round button with a power symbol (circle around a line).
2. Press the power button once. The camera will turn on and the lens will extend to shooting position. The LCD screen will light up, displaying the shooting screen.

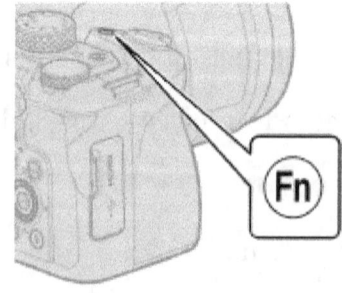

Turning Off:

1. Locate the power button again.
2. Press and hold the power button for a moment. You might see a confirmation prompt on the LCD screen (depending on your camera settings).
3. Release the button when the camera powers off and the lens retracts.

Additional Notes:

- The camera might also turn off automatically after a period of inactivity to conserve battery life. You can adjust the auto-off time in the camera's menu settings.
- If the lens encounters any resistance while extending or retracting, the camera might turn off automatically as a safety precaution. Check for any objects obstructing the lens and try turning the camera on again.

By following these simple steps, you can power your Nikon Coolpix P950 on and off for effortless shooting.

Setting the Date and Time

Here's how to set the date and time on your Nikon Coolpix P950:

1. Access the Menu:

- Turn on your Nikon Coolpix P950 if it's not already on.
- Locate the **Menu button**(usually labelled with the word "Menu" or lines). It's often on the back of the camera, near the bottom right corner.
- Press the **Menu button** to display the camera's menu options on the LCD screen.

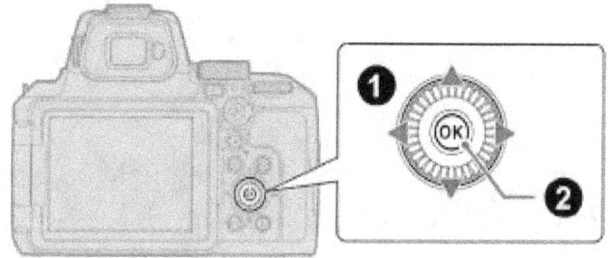

2. Navigate to the Setup Menu:

- The menu options might be displayed in a tabbed interface. Use the multi selector (the four-directional buttons on the back of the camera) to navigate through the tabs.

- Look for a tab labelled **Setup**, **Settings**, or similar.

- Press the multi selector right button to enter the Setup menu.

3. Find the Date and Time Option:

- Once you're in the Setup menu, scroll through the options using the up and down buttons of the multi selector.

- Look for an option labelled **Date and Time**, **Time Zone and Date**, or similar.

- When you find the date and time setting, press the multi selector right button to enter it.

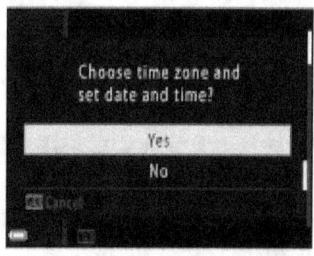

4. Set the Date and Time:

- You'll likely see separate fields for year, month, day, hour, minute, and time zone (optional).

- Use the multi selector buttons to highlight each field you want to change.

- Use the dial (usually located on the top right of the camera) or the up/down buttons of the multi selector to adjust the values.

- A confirmation prompt might appear after setting each value.

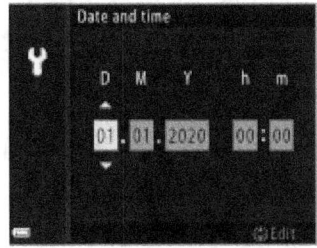

5. Apply the Settings and Exit:

- Once you've set the desired date, time, and optionally the time zone, navigate to the "**OK**" or "**Confirm**" option (usually highlighted in colour).

- Press the multi selector right button to confirm and save the settings.

- Press the **Menu button** repeatedly to exit the menu and return to the shooting screen.

Additional Notes:

- Consult your camera's manual for specific instructions and menu navigation details, as the wording of menu options might vary slightly depending on the camera model and firmware version.

- Some Nikon Coolpix models might offer the option to set the time zone based on your home city or a travel destination. Explore the time zone settings if available.

By following these steps, you can ensure your Nikon Coolpix P950 captures images and videos with accurate timestamps.

The Menu System

The Nikon Coolpix P950's menu system provides access to various camera settings and functionalities. Here's a breakdown of its structure and navigation:

Accessing the Menu:

- Locate the **Menu button** on the back of the camera, typically near the bottom right corner. It's usually labelled with the word "Menu" or has lines on it.

- Press the **Menu button** to display the camera's menu options on the LCD screen.

Menu Layout:

The menu layout might involve tabs or categories depending on the camera model and firmware version. Here's a general overview:

- **Tabs (if applicable):** Some Coolpix models might have a tabbed interface where you navigate between sections like Shooting Menu, Playback Menu, Setup Menu, etc., using the multi selector left/right buttons.

- **Menu Categories:** Within each tab or directly on the main menu screen (if no tabs are present), you'll see a list of menu categories represented by icons and labels.

Navigating the Menu:

- Use the **multi selector** (the four-directional buttons on the back of the camera) to navigate through the menu options.

- **Up/Down buttons:** Move the highlight up or down to browse through different menu categories or settings within a sub-menu.

- **Right button:** Press the multi selector right button to enter a highlighted menu category and access its sub-options.

- **Left button (or Back button):** Press the multi selector left button (or a dedicated Back button if present) to go back to the previous menu level.

Making Selections and Adjustments:

- Once you enter a sub-menu with specific settings, you can use the multi selector buttons to highlight the setting you want to adjust.

- The **dial** (usually located on the top right of the camera) or the **up/down buttons** of the multi selector can be used to change the value or setting of the highlighted option.

- Some settings might offer a visual representation or a brief explanation when highlighted.

Exiting the Menu:

- Press the **Menu button** repeatedly to exit sub-menus and return to the main shooting screen.

Common Menu Categories (may vary slightly depending on the model):

- **Shooting Menu:** Controls related to shooting modes, picture quality, exposure compensation, white balance, focus, etc.

- **Playback Menu:** Options for reviewing captured photos and videos, image playback zoom, deleting images, slideshows, etc.

- **Setup Menu:** Settings for date and time, auto-off, formatting memory cards, language, reset options, and other camera functions.

- **Movie Menu (on some models):** Settings specifically for video recording, like video resolution, frame rate, and microphone settings.

Additional Tips:

- Consult your camera's manual for specific details and explanations of each menu option, as the exact wording and layout might vary slightly depending on the model and firmware version.
- Some menu options might have sub-menus with further controls. Explore the menus to familiarize yourself with all the available settings.
- The camera might display a brief description of the highlighted setting for your reference.

By understanding the menu system and using the navigation tips, you can explore the various settings on your Nikon Coolpix P950 and customize it to suit your shooting preferences.

CHAPTER THREE
SHOOTING MODES

Auto Mode

The Nikon Coolpix P950's Auto mode, also sometimes called "Standard Auto" or "Easy Auto," is designed for simple point-and-shoot photography. It's a great option for beginners or when you want the camera to handle most settings automatically.

What it Does:

- **Scene Detection:** The camera analyses the shooting scene and automatically selects the most appropriate shooting mode from its repertoire. This could be Landscape mode, Portrait mode, Close-up mode, or something else depending on the subject and lighting conditions.

- **Exposure Control:** The camera automatically sets the shutter speed and aperture to achieve a balanced exposure for the scene.

- **Focus:** Auto mode uses autofocus to lock onto the main subject and achieve sharp focus.

- **Flash:** The camera decides whether to fire the flash based on the lighting conditions and scene analysis. In some situations, it might use red-eye reduction when the flash fires.

The Auto shooting option is ideal for rapid shots during fast-paced situations where time is limited.

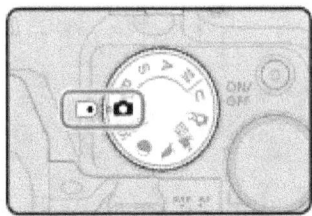

Select this mode for general shooting in a variety of conditions.

In auto mode, the camera detects the main subject and focuses on it using target finding AF. If a human face is detected, the camera automatically prioritizes focus on the face.

Features Available in Auto Mode

- **Autofocus**
    - Using autofocus

- **Flash Mode**
  - Setting the flash mode
- **Self-timer**
  - Using the self-timer
- **Smile Timer**
  - Using the smile timer
- **Focus Mode**
  - Selecting the focus mode
- **Exposure Compensation**
  - Adjusting exposure compensation
- **Shooting Menu**
  - Accessing the shooting menu (common across all shooting modes)

Benefits of Using Auto Mode:

- **Simple and Easy to Use:** Ideal for beginners or casual photographers who don't want to worry about complex camera settings.
- **Convenient for Various Situations:** The camera adapts to different shooting scenarios, making it versatile for everyday photography.
- **Reliable Results:** In most well-lit situations, Auto mode can capture good quality images with proper exposure and focus.

Limitations of Auto Mode:

- **Less Creative Control:** You give up control over shutter speed, aperture, ISO, and other settings that can be used for creative effects.
- **Potentially Not Ideal for All Situations:** Auto mode might not always choose the best settings for challenging lighting conditions, fast-moving subjects, or creative effects.

When to Use Auto Mode:

- **Everyday Snapshots:** For capturing everyday moments, events, or scenery without worrying about settings.
- **Travel Photography:** When you're traveling and want to capture various sights without getting bogged down in camera adjustments.

- **Low-Light Situations (with limitations):** Auto mode can adjust for some low-light situations, but might not always produce the best results.

Moving Beyond Auto Mode:

- As you gain confidence with your camera, you can experiment with other shooting modes on the Coolpix P950 that offer more creative control over settings like aperture priority, shutter priority, or manual mode.

- Consult your camera's manual to understand these modes and how to use them to achieve your desired creative effects.

In summary, the Nikon Coolpix P950's Auto mode is a user-friendly option for capturing everyday photos with ease. However, if you want to explore creative photography or have more control over your images, venturing beyond Auto mode and into the camera's other shooting modes is recommended.

Scene Modes

The Nikon Coolpix P950 offers various Scene Modes to optimize camera settings for specific shooting situations. Here's a breakdown of some common Scene Modes along with illustrative diagrams:

1. Portrait Mode (Icon: Person's face):

- Use this mode for capturing well-exposed and focused portraits of people.
- The camera prioritizes focus on the subject's face and might apply skin softening (on some models) for a smoother complexion.

2. Landscape Mode (Icon: Mountainscape):

- Ideal for capturing photos of landscapes, seascapes, or cityscapes.
- The camera sets a wider aperture (smaller f-number) to ensure maximum depth of field, keeping both foreground and background elements in focus.

3. Night Landscape Mode (Icon: Cityscape at night):

- Designed for capturing nighttime scenes with minimal noise or blur.
- The camera uses a slower shutter speed to capture more light but might require a tripod for stability to avoid camera shake.

4. Close-up Mode (Icon: Flower):

- Use this mode for capturing close-up photos of flowers, insects, or small objects.
- The camera sets a focus distance appropriate for macro photography and might use a larger aperture (smaller f-number) for a shallow depth of field, potentially blurring the background behind the subject.

5. Beach/Snow Mode (Icon: Palm tree and sun):

- Suitable for capturing photos on beaches or in snowy conditions.
- The camera adjusts white balance to compensate for the bright, reflective nature of sand or snow and ensure accurate color reproduction.

6. Sports Mode (Icon: Person running):

- Designed for capturing fast-moving action, such as sports or wildlife.
- The camera uses a faster shutter speed to freeze the action and minimize motion blur.

7. Party/Indoor Mode (Icon: People at a party):

- Use this mode for capturing photos in low-light indoor environments, such as parties or concerts.
- The camera increases the ISO sensitivity to capture more light but might introduce some image noise. The flash might also fire automatically.

8. Sunset Mode (Icon: Sun setting over horizon):

- Ideal for capturing sunsets or sunrises.
- The camera adjusts white balance and exposure to enhance the warm colours of the sky.

9. Bird-Watching Mode (Icon: Bird):

- Designed for photographing birds in their natural habitat.
- The camera uses a faster zoom setting and might adjust focus settings to help capture distant birds.

10. Moon Mode (Icon: Moon):

- Use this mode for capturing photos of the moon.
- The camera adjusts settings to achieve a clear image of the moon, potentially using a slower shutter speed and a small aperture. A tripod is recommended for stability.

These are just some of the common Scene Modes available on the Nikon Coolpix P950. Consult your camera's manual for a complete list of Scene Modes and their specific functions. By understanding these modes and their uses, you can choose the appropriate one to optimize your camera settings for the scene you're capturing.

P, S, A, and M Modes (Program, Shutter Priority, Aperture Priority, Manual)

Before diving into the specific modes, it's helpful to understand the concept of exposure, which is the foundation of these shooting modes. Proper exposure refers to an image that's not too bright (overexposed) or too dark (underexposed). Imagine exposure like a recipe; you need the right balance of ingredients (light) to create a perfect dish (photo).

Three elements play a vital role in achieving correct exposure:

1. **Aperture:** The aperture of your camera lens acts like the iris of your eye, controlling the amount of light that enters the sensor. A wider aperture (smaller f-number) lets in more light, while a narrower aperture (larger f-number) lets in less light.

2. **Shutter Speed:** This controls the duration of time the camera's sensor is exposed to light. A slower shutter speed allows more light to enter the sensor but can cause motion blur if the camera or subject moves. A faster shutter speed captures sharper images of moving subjects but lets in less light.

3. **ISO:** ISO refers to the sensor's sensitivity to light. A higher ISO setting increases sensitivity but can introduce unwanted image noise (grain) in low-light situations.

These three elements work together to influence the final exposure of your image. The camera's meter constantly measures incoming light and tries to achieve a balanced exposure by adjusting these settings automatically in some modes or manually by you in others.

Nikon Coolpix P950 Shooting Modes: P, S, A, and M

The Nikon Coolpix P950 offers several shooting modes that provide varying levels of control over these exposure settings:

1. Program Mode (P Mode) -

- **Function:** Program mode is a good starting point for beginners or everyday shooting. The camera automatically sets both aperture and shutter speed for a balanced exposure in most situations.

- **Use Case:** Ideal for capturing everyday photos, snapshots, or when you want the camera to handle most settings automatically.

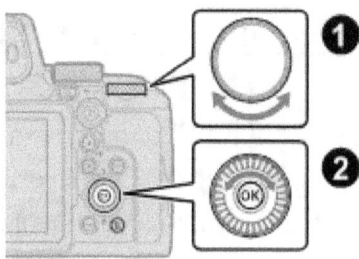

2. Shutter Priority Mode (S Mode) -

- **Function:** In Shutter Priority mode, you choose the desired shutter speed, and the camera automatically adjusts the aperture to achieve correct exposure. This mode is helpful for capturing specific effects:
    - **Faster shutter speeds:** Freeze action for moving subjects like sports or wildlife.
    - **Slower shutter speeds:** Create motion blur for artistic effects like waterfalls or light trails at night (requires a tripod for stability).
- **Use Case:** Ideal for capturing sharp action shots or creative motion blur effects.

3. Aperture Priority Mode (A Mode) -

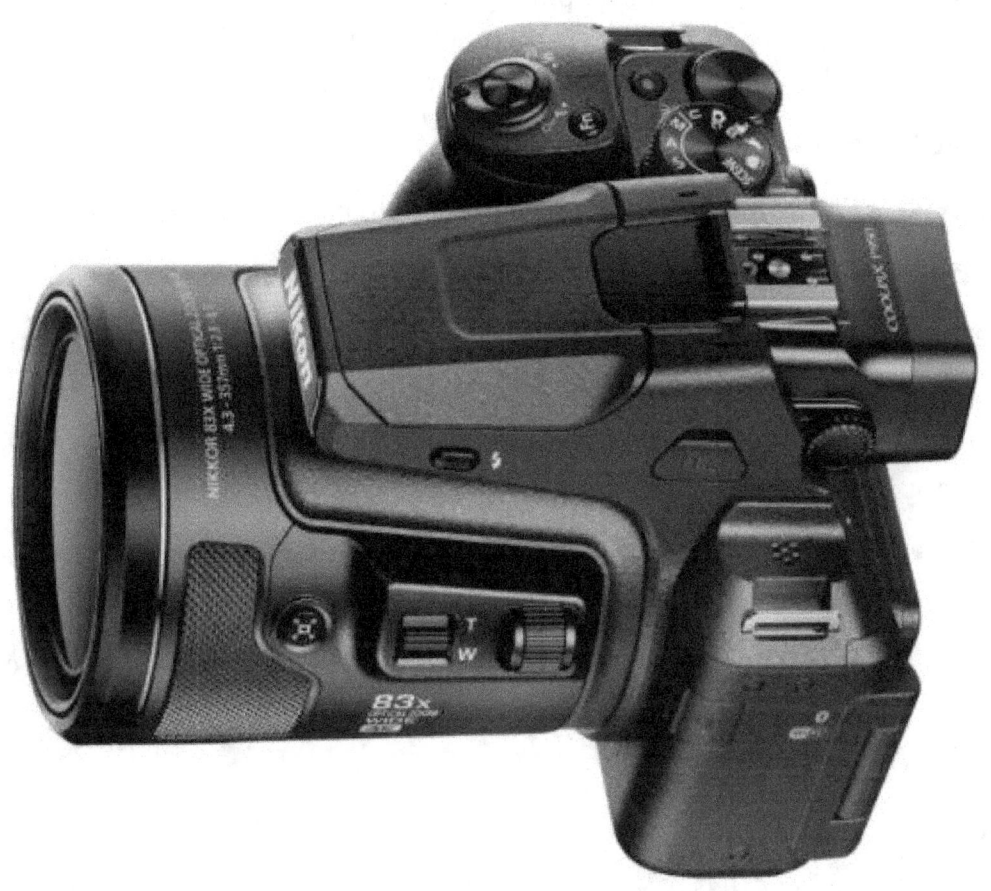

- **Function:** In Aperture Priority mode, you select the desired aperture, and the camera automatically adjusts the shutter speed for balanced exposure. This mode is useful for controlling depth of field:
    - **Wider aperture (smaller f-number):** Creates a shallow depth of field, blurring the background and isolating your subject (ideal for portraits).
    - **Narrower aperture (larger f-number):** Creates a deeper depth of field, keeping both foreground and background elements in focus (ideal for landscapes).
- **Use Case:** Suitable for controlling depth of field for creative effects like portraiture or landscape photography.

4. **Manual Mode (M Mode) -**

- **Function:** Manual mode provides complete control over shutter speed, aperture, and ISO. You make all the adjustments to achieve the desired exposure and creative effects. A good understanding of exposure is essential for using this mode effectively.

- **Use Case:** Ideal for experienced photographers who want full creative control over their images or situations where automatic modes might struggle, like low-light photography with specific shutter speed or aperture requirements.

Choosing the Right Mode:

- **Beginners:** Start with Program mode (P) for automatic operation.
- **Everyday Shooting:** Use Program mode (P) for convenience.
- **Action or Motion Blur:** Use Shutter Priority mode (S) for creative control over shutter speed.
- **Depth of Field Control:** Use Aperture Priority mode (A) to manage foreground and background blur.
- **Full Creative Control:** Use Manual mode (M) for experienced photographers who understand exposure.

By understanding these shooting modes and how they influence exposure, you can choose the best option for your desired creative effects or shooting scenarios with your Nikon Coolpix P950.

Movie Mode

The Nikon Coolpix P950 offers a Movie mode for recording videos with various options to suit your needs. Here's a breakdown of Movie mode on the Coolpix P950:

Accessing Movie Mode:

- The method to access Movie mode might vary slightly depending on your camera model. In general, you can find the Movie mode option on the camera's mode dial or shooting menu. Look for an icon that resembles a movie camera.

Recording Video:

1. Once you've entered Movie mode, you'll see the live view on the camera's screen with movie recording options displayed.
2. Compose your shot and ensure your subject is in focus.
3. Press the record button (usually a red button) to start recording. A timer will indicate the recording duration on the screen.
4. Press the record button again to stop recording. The camera will process and save the video file.

Movie Recording Options:

- **Movie Resolution and Frame Rate:** The Coolpix P950 allows you to choose different video resolutions and frame rates. Higher resolutions (like 4K UHD) offer sharper video quality but take up more storage space. Higher frame rates (like 60p) create smoother slow-motion effects but also require more storage. Choose the option that balances quality and storage capacity based on your needs.

- **Electronic VR (Image Stabilization):** This feature helps minimize camera shake during video recording, resulting in smoother footage. It's recommended to keep it enabled for sharper videos, especially when shooting handheld.

- **Focus Mode:** You can choose between autofocus (camera automatically focuses) or manual focus (you adjust the focus ring on the lens) for video recording. Autofocus is generally convenient, while manual focus might be beneficial for specific creative effects.

- **Zoom:** The Coolpix P950 allows zooming while recording a video, but zooming in and out can be jerky or cause autofocus hunting (camera constantly refocusing). It's recommended to zoom to your desired focal length before starting the recording.

Additional Considerations:

- **Memory Card:** Movie files can be large, especially at higher resolutions. Ensure you have a fast memory card (SDHC or SDXC with UHS Speed Class 1 or higher) for smooth recording and playback.

- **Battery Life:** Video recording consumes more battery power than photo shooting. Carry a spare battery if you plan on extensive video recording sessions.

- **External Microphone (Optional):** The Coolpix P950 might allow connecting an external microphone for improved audio quality in your videos (refer to your camera's manual for compatibility).

Using Movie Mode Effectively:

- Think about the story you want to tell with your video before recording.
- Maintain stable handholding or use a tripod for smoother footage.
- Experiment with different angles and compositions to add visual interest.
- Pay attention to lighting and sound quality for better results.

By understanding the Movie mode functions and options on your Nikon Coolpix P950, you can capture high-quality videos for your memories or creative projects.

CHAPTER FOUR
TAKING PICTURES

Using the Zoom Lens

When you move the zoom control, the zoom lens position changes.

- **To zoom in (telephoto position)**: Move the control toward **T**.

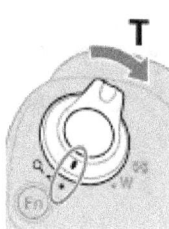

- **To zoom out (wide-angle position)**: Move the control toward **W**.

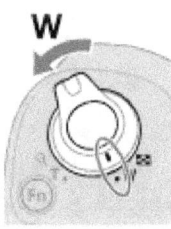

Rotating the zoom control all the way in either direction adjusts the zoom quickly.

The zoom indicator and focal length (in 35mm [135] format) are displayed on the shooting screen when the zoom control is moved.

Digital zoom (2), which allows you to further magnify the subject up to approximately 4× the maximum optical zoom ratio, can be activated by moving and holding the zoom control toward **T** when the camera is zoomed in to the maximum optical zoom position (1).

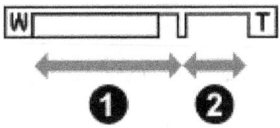

Zooming Tips:

- **Compose Your Shot First:** Frame your image at the wide-angle position before zooming in. This helps you locate and position your subject within the frame.

- **Use the Viewfinder (Optional):** For more precise framing and stability, especially when zoomed in considerably, consider using the camera's viewfinder instead of the LCD screen.

- **Stability is Key:** Camera shake becomes more prominent at high zoom levels. Use a tripod or a stable surface to support the camera and avoid blurry images.

- **Focus and Refocus:** As you zoom, the camera might need to refocus to maintain image sharpness. Half-pressing the shutter button (without fully taking the picture) can trigger autofocus before capturing the image.

- **Digital Zoom (Optional):** The Coolpix P950 might offer a digital zoom option that extends the zoom range beyond the optical zoom limit. However, digital zoom reduces image quality, so use it sparingly.

Focusing

The Nikon Coolpix P950 offers various focusing options to ensure your subject appears sharp and crisp in your photos. Here's a breakdown of focusing modes and techniques for achieving accurate focus:

Understanding Focus:

- In photography, focusing refers to the process of adjusting the camera lens to achieve optimal sharpness on your chosen subject. A properly focused image will have clear details, while an out-of-focus image will appear blurry or soft.

Focusing Modes on the Coolpix P950:

- **Autofocus (AF):** This is the most common mode, where the camera automatically detects and focuses on the subject. It's convenient for everyday shooting and beginners.
    - **Subject Detection AF:** The camera analyzes the scene and identifies the main subject, prioritizing focus on it.
    - **Face Detection AF:** This mode prioritizes focusing on faces within the frame, ideal for portraits.

- **Manual Focus (MF):** In this mode, you manually adjust the focus ring on the lens to achieve sharp focus on your desired point. It offers more precise control but requires practice.

Selecting the Focus Mode:

- The Coolpix P950 usually has a dedicated focus mode button or allows you to choose the mode through the camera menu (consult your camera's manual for specifics).

Focusing Techniques:

- **Half-Press Shutter Button:** When using Autofocus, half-pressing the shutter button down halfway activates autofocus. The camera will focus on the subject in the centre of the frame by default. Once focused, a green focus confirmation indicator will appear in the viewfinder or LCD screen.

- **Focus Lock (Optional):** Some Coolpix models might offer a focus lock function. After achieving focus with a half-press, you can press a specific button (check your manual) to lock focus, allowing you to recompose the image before taking the picture.

- **Focus Point Selection (Optional):** Some Coolpix models allow selecting a specific focus point within the frame instead of relying on the centre focus point. This can be useful for off-centre compositions.

Focusing Tips:

- **Subject Contrast:** The camera's autofocus system relies on contrast to detect edges and achieve focus. Subjects with high contrast (dark clothes against a light background) are easier for the camera to focus on compared to low-contrast subjects (solid colour walls).

- **Focus Distance:** Ensure you're within the minimum focusing distance of your lens to achieve sharp focus. Refer to your camera's manual for this specification.

- **Continuous Shooting (Optional):** For capturing moving subjects, consider using continuous shooting mode (where the camera takes multiple pictures in rapid succession). Autofocus might continuously adjust during continuous shooting to track the moving subject.

- **Manual Focus Practice:** If you're interested in more creative control, experiment with manual focus. Use the focus ring to achieve sharp focus on your desired subject area.

By understanding the focusing modes and techniques available on your Nikon Coolpix P950, you can ensure your photos capture your subjects in perfect clarity, adding a professional touch to your images.

Exposure Basics (Aperture, Shutter Speed, ISO)

Aperture, shutter speed, and ISO are the three fundamental aspects that control exposure in photography, working together to determine how much light reaches the camera's sensor and ultimately affecting the brightness of your image.

Here's a breakdown of each element and its impact on exposure:

1. Aperture:

- Imagine the aperture as the iris of your eye. It controls the size of the opening in the lens that allows light to enter the camera sensor. Aperture is denoted by an f-number (e.g., f/2.8, f/8, f/16).

- **Larger Aperture (smaller f-number):** This allows more light to enter the sensor in a shorter amount of time. Results in:
    - Brighter images (useful in low-light situations)
    - shallower depth of field (background blur) - ideal for isolating your subject.

- **Smaller Aperture (larger f-number):** This allows less light to enter the sensor, requiring a slower shutter speed or higher ISO for proper exposure. Results in:
    - Darker images (may require additional light or camera adjustments)
    - Deeper depth of field (more of the scene appears in focus) - ideal for landscapes.

2. Shutter Speed:

- Shutter speed refers to the duration of time the camera's sensor is exposed to light. It's measured in fractions of a second (e.g., 1/1000s, 1/250s, 1/2s).

- **Faster Shutter Speed:** This captures a shorter slice of time, freezing motion. Results in:
    - Sharper images of moving subjects (ideal for sports or wildlife)
    - Darker images (less light reaches the sensor)

- **Slower Shutter Speed:** This allows more light to reach the sensor but increases the risk of camera shake or subject blur if moving. Results in:
    - Brighter images (more light captured)
    - Blurry images (if camera or subject moves) - may require a tripod for stability in low light.

3. ISO:

- ISO refers to the sensor's sensitivity to light. It's similar to the ISO setting on film photography. A higher ISO setting increases the sensor's sensitivity, allowing you to capture images in low-light conditions without needing a slower shutter speed or wider aperture. However, higher ISO also introduces unwanted image noise (grain) in the photo.
- **Lower ISO:** This setting is ideal for well-lit situations, producing images with minimal noise.
- **Higher ISO:** This setting allows you to capture images in low light but can introduce noticeable grain in the image.

The Balancing Act:

These three elements work together to influence the final exposure of your image. Ideally, you want a balanced exposure where your image is neither too bright (overexposed) nor too dark (underexposed). You can adjust these settings in your camera to achieve the desired effect for your photos.

Here's an analogy: Imagine you're trying to fill a bucket with water.

- **Aperture** is the size of the hole in the bucket. A larger hole (wider aperture) lets more water (light) in quickly.
- **Shutter Speed** is the length of time the hole is open. A longer time (slower shutter speed) allows more water (light) to enter.
- **ISO** is like adding a water pump. A higher ISO setting pumps water (increases light sensitivity) faster, but it might also stir up dirt (introduce image noise).

By adjusting these settings, you can control how much and how quickly light fills the bucket (sensor) to achieve a perfectly exposed image.

Additional Tips:

- Many cameras offer an automatic mode that sets these elements for you. It's a good starting point, but for more creative control, consider switching to shutter priority, aperture priority, or manual mode where you can adjust these settings yourself.
- Experiment with different combinations of aperture, shutter speed, and ISO to see how they affect your photos. There's no one-size-fits-all solution; the best settings depend on the lighting conditions and the creative effect you're aiming for.

By understanding these exposure basics, you'll be well on your way to capturing beautiful, well-exposed photos with your Nikon Coolpix P950.

White Balance

In photography, white balance (WB) plays a crucial role in ensuring the colours in your image appear natural and accurate. Imagine taking a picture of a white shirt under different light sources; it might appear yellowish under incandescent bulbs or slightly bluish under daylight. White balance corrects for these colour casts, making the white shirt appear truly white in the final image.

Understanding Colour Temperature:

- Light sources have varying colour temperatures measured in Kelvins (K). A lower Kelvin temperature represents a warmer light source (like incandescent bulbs), while a higher Kelvin temperature represents a cooler light source (like daylight or shade).

Impact of colour Temperature on Images:

- When you take a picture under a specific light source, the camera sensor captures the light and interprets the colour temperature. If not corrected, the captured colours might have a slight cast depending on the light source.

White Balance Settings on the Nikon Coolpix P950:

Your Coolpix P950 offers various white balance settings to optimize colour reproduction for different lighting conditions:

- **Auto White Balance (AWB):** This is the most common setting. The camera automatically analyses the light source and attempts to set a neutral white balance for a natural look. AWB works well under most lighting conditions, but it might not always be perfect.
- **Incandescent:** Use this setting for pictures taken under indoor lighting with incandescent bulbs, which have a warm colour temperature. It corrects for the yellow cast and produces more natural-looking colours.
- **Fluorescent:** This setting is suitable for pictures taken under fluorescent lights, which often have a greenish cast. It counteracts the green tint and delivers more accurate colours.
- **Cloudy:** Use this setting for pictures taken on cloudy days when the light appears cooler. It warms up the image slightly for a more natural look.
- **Sunny:** This setting is suitable for pictures taken outdoors on sunny days when the light is bright and cool. It cools down the image slightly for a more natural look.
- **Preset White Balance:** Some Coolpix models might offer additional presets like Flash, Shade, or Custom, allowing you to choose based on the specific lighting situation.
- **Manual White Balance:** For experienced photographers, this mode allows setting a custom white balance using a white balance card under the same lighting conditions as your subject. This can provide the most accurate colour reproduction.

Choosing the Right White Balance:

- The appropriate white balance setting depends on the lighting conditions when you capture the image.
- If you're unsure, start with Auto White Balance (AWB) and adjust it later during post-processing on a computer if necessary.

Additional Tips:

- Shooting in RAW format allows more flexibility for adjusting white balance in post-processing software compared to JPEG.
- A white balance card can be a valuable tool for setting a custom white balance, especially in challenging lighting situations.

By understanding white balance and using the appropriate settings on your Nikon Coolpix P950, you can capture images with natural and accurate colours, enhancing the overall quality and realism of your photos.

Metering Modes

Your Nikon Coolpix P950 offers various metering modes to determine how the camera measures light and sets the exposure for your photos. Understanding these modes will help you achieve balanced and properly exposed images in different shooting scenarios.

What is Metering?

Metering refers to the process by which your camera measures the light entering the lens and determines the appropriate shutter speed and aperture combination to achieve a correctly exposed image. A well-exposed image is neither too bright (overexposed) nor too dark (underexposed).

Metering Modes on the Nikon Coolpix P950:

The Nikon Coolpix P950 typically offers these metering modes:

- **Matrix Metering (Multi-pattern Metering):** This is the default mode on most Coolpix cameras. The camera divides the frame into several zones and measures the light in each zone. It then calculates an average exposure for the entire scene, considering highlights and shadows. This mode is versatile and works well in various lighting conditions.
- **Centre-Weighted Metering:** In this mode, the camera prioritizes the light reading from the centre of the frame, where your subject is most likely to be positioned. This mode is suitable for situations with evenly lit backgrounds or when your main subject occupies a significant portion of the frame.

- **Spot Metering:** This mode measures the light from a very small, specific area of the frame. You can use the camera's focus point to determine the metering spot. This mode is useful for high-contrast scenes where the background is much brighter or darker than your subject. By spot metering on your subject, you can ensure it's properly exposed even if the background is over or underexposed.

Choosing the Right Metering Mode:

- **Matrix Metering:** A good starting point for most situations. It considers various lighting zones for a balanced exposure.

- **Centre-Weighted Metering:** Use this when your subject is in the centre of the frame and the background has similar lighting.

- **Spot Metering:** Ideal for high-contrast scenes or when you want precise exposure control over a specific area, like a backlit subject.

Here are some additional factors to consider when choosing a metering mode:

- **Lighting Conditions:** Matrix metering is good for balanced lighting. In high-contrast situations, consider spot metering for better subject exposure.

- **Subject Placement:** If your subject is off-centre, centre-weighted metering might not prioritize it correctly. Spot metering can help in such scenarios.

Metering and Exposure Compensation:

- Even with the chosen metering mode, the camera's automatic exposure might not always be perfect. You can use Exposure Compensation to adjust the camera's suggested exposure if the image appears too bright or too dark.

By understanding metering modes and their applications on your Nikon Coolpix P950, you can take more control over how the camera measures light and achieve optimal exposure for your desired results.

Using the Flash

The built-in flash on your Nikon Coolpix P950 can be a helpful tool for illuminating your subject in low-light conditions. Here's a breakdown of using the flash effectively, along with safety precautions:

Activating the Flash:

- The method to activate the flash might vary slightly depending on your specific Coolpix model. In general, you'll find a dedicated flash button on the top of the camera, usually next to the shutter release button.

- Pressing this button typically pops up the flash unit from its retracted position.

Flash Modes:

Your Coolpix P950 likely offers several flash modes to control how the flash fires:

- **Auto Flash:** This is the most common mode. The camera automatically decides whether to fire the flash based on the lighting conditions.
- **Fill Flash:** Even in daylight situations, you might use fill flash to add light to your subject, especially when there are harsh shadows on the face (portraits) or the background is much brighter than the subject.
- **Red-Eye Reduction:** This mode fires a pre-flash before the main flash to reduce the red-eye effect that can sometimes appear in portraits due to light reflecting off the subject's retinas.
- **Slow Synchro (Rear-Curtain Sync):** This mode can be used for creative effects in low-light situations. The flash fires at the end of the exposure, potentially creating streaks of light from moving objects (like people walking) while the shutter remains open.

Using the Flash Effectively:

- **Flash Range:** The flash on your Coolpix P950 has a limited range. Consult your camera's manual to know the effective distance for proper illumination of your subject.
- **Direct Flash vs. Bounced Flash:** Direct flash can sometimes create harsh shadows. You can soften the light by bouncing the flash off a ceiling or wall (if available). Some Coolpix models might have a built-in diffuser that scatters the light for a softer effect.
- **Red-Eye Reduction:** While helpful, red-eye reduction might slightly slow down camera response. If red-eye isn't a major concern, you can use the regular flash mode for faster shooting.

Safety Precautions:

- **Don't use the flash too close to your subject:** At very close distances, the flash can cause glare or unnatural-looking lighting on your subject.
- **Be aware of reflective surfaces:** Flash can bounce off reflective surfaces like mirrors or windows, creating unwanted glare in your image.

By understanding how to use the flash and its different modes on your Nikon Coolpix P950, you can add light to your photos in low-light situations and achieve more creative effects with your flash photography.

Reviewing Images

The Nikon Coolpix P950 offers several ways to review the images and videos you've captured. Here's a guide on how to access and navigate your captured media:

Playback Mode:

- Press the playback button (usually a button with a play icon) to enter playback mode. This mode allows you to view your photos and videos on the camera's LCD screen.

Reviewing Images:

- Use the multi-selector on the back of the camera to navigate through your images. Pressing up or down will move between images, while pressing left or right might cycle through different playback options depending on your camera model.

- The zoom control (usually a rocker switch on top) can be used to zoom in and out on an image for closer inspection of details.

Playback Information:

- While reviewing images, you might see information overlaid on the screen, such as:
  - Filename
  - Date and time the image was captured
  - Exposure information (aperture, shutter speed, ISO)

- You can usually press a designated button (check your camera's manual) to toggle the display of this information on or off.

Additional Playback Options:

- **Slideshow:** Some Coolpix models might offer a slideshow option to automatically play back your images in sequence on the LCD screen.

- **Image Playback Options:** You might be able to access a menu with options like:
  - Rotate images (correcting tilted shots)
  - Apply basic image edits (e.g., cropping, color adjustments) - these edits might not be saved permanently on the original image file.
  - Delete unwanted images (use caution as deleted images are typically unrecoverable)

Reviewing Videos:

- In playback mode, videos are usually indicated by a play icon or a different thumbnail layout compared to images.
- Select the video you want to play, and press the play button to start playback.
- Playback controls might appear on the screen, allowing you to pause, rewind, or fast-forward through the video.
- You might also be able to adjust the volume during video playback.

Connecting to a Computer or TV:

- For a larger viewing experience or to transfer your images and videos to a computer for editing or sharing, you can connect your Coolpix P950:
    - **To a computer:** Use a USB cable to connect the camera to your computer. Your computer might recognize the camera as a removable disk, allowing you to access your photos and videos for transfer.
    - **To a TV:** Some Coolpix models might have a built-in HDMI port or offer an optional AV cable. Connect the camera to your TV using the appropriate cable, and navigate the camera's playback mode to display images and videos on the TV screen.

By understanding the playback options and functionalities of your Nikon Coolpix P950, you can effectively review your captured memories and share them with others. Refer to your camera's manual for specific details and button functions for your particular model.

CHAPTER FIVE
PLAYBACK AND EDITING

Playing Back Images

1. Press the Playback button to enter full-frame playback mode.

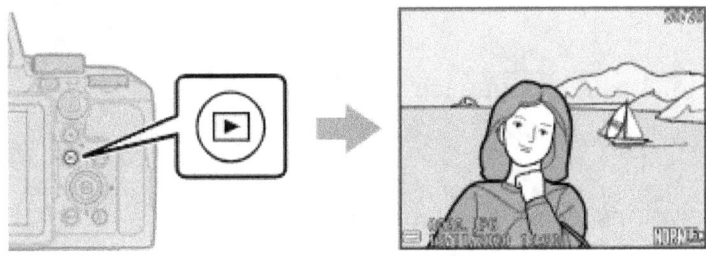

- If you press and hold down the Playback button while the camera is turned off, it will turn on in playback mode. Use the multi selector to choose an image to display.

2. Use the multi selector ◄ to display the previous image or ► to display the next image. Press and hold down either direction to scroll through the images quickly. You can also select images by rotating the multi selector.

- Press the Display button to cycle through the information displayed on the screen.

- To play back a recorded movie, press the OK button.

- To return to shooting mode, press the Playback button or the shutter-release button.

- Move the zoom control toward T (Telephoto) in full-frame playback mode to zoom in on an image (playback zoom).

- In full-frame playback mode, move the zoom control toward W (Wide-angle) to switch to thumbnail playback mode and display multiple images on the screen (thumbnail playback/calendar display).

Other Playback Methods

- Easy Panorama
    - Playback with easy panorama
- Sequence Images
    - Viewing images in a sequence
- Movies
    - Basic operations of movie recording and playback
    - Operations during movie playback

Deleting Images

1. In playback mode, press the Delete button to delete the image currently displayed on the screen.

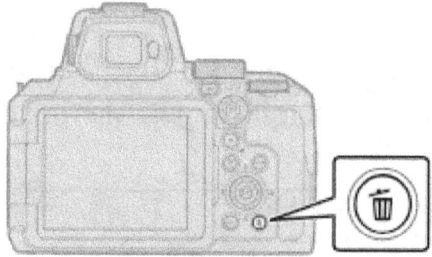

2. Use the multi selector to choose the desired deletion method and press the OK button.

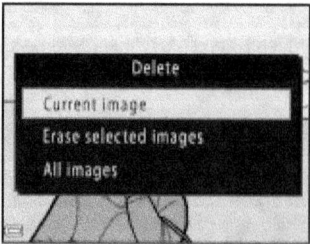

- If you selected [Current image] or [All images], proceed to step 6.
- To exit without deleting, press the Back button.

3. Use the multi selector or rotate it to select the image you want to delete.

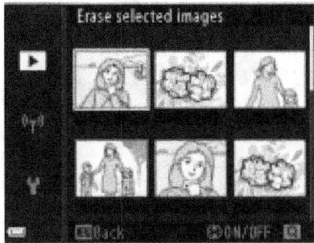

- Move the zoom control toward T (Telephoto) to switch to full-frame playback or toward W (Wide-angle) to switch to thumbnail playback.

4. Use the multi selector to show or hide the delete icon.

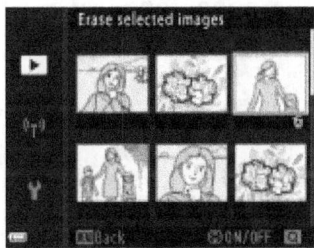

- Show the delete icon under images that you want to delete. Repeat steps 3 and 4 to select additional images.

5. Press the OK button to apply the image selection.

6. When the confirmation dialog appears, select [Yes] and press the OK button.

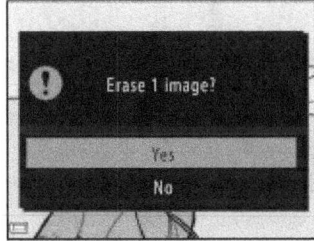

- Deleted images cannot be recovered.
- The message in the confirmation dialog will vary depending on the selected deletion method.

In-Camera Editing

The Nikon Coolpix P950 offers limited in-camera editing capabilities compared to software like Photoshop or even some mobile editing apps. However, it does provide some basic editing functions you can use to enhance your photos directly on the camera. Here's what you can do:

Basic Trimming: You can trim unwanted portions from a captured image. This is useful for removing unnecessary background elements or adjusting the composition slightly.

Red-Eye Correction: The camera can automatically detect and reduce the appearance of red-eye in portraits caused by the camera flash reflecting off people's eyes.

D-Lighting: D-Lighting is a Nikon feature that helps recover details in shadow areas of an image. This can be beneficial for underexposed photos where shadows appear too dark. Be careful not to overuse D-Lighting, as it can create an unnatural look in some situations.

Skin Softening (Optional): Some Nikon Coolpix models might offer a "Skin Softening" option for portrait photos. This can reduce the appearance of wrinkles and blemishes for a smoother complexion. However, use this function sparingly to avoid an overly artificial look.

Filter Effects: The camera might offer a variety of creative filter effects that you can apply to your photos for artistic expression. These filters can alter the colour tone, saturation, or add specific effects like black and white or miniature.

Resizing Images: You can resize captured images to a smaller resolution within the camera. This can be helpful for saving storage space on your memory card or emailing photos. However, keep in mind that resizing reduces image quality, so it's best to resize only when necessary.

Cropping: Similar to trimming, you can crop an image to a specific size or aspect ratio. This allows you to focus on a particular element within the frame or adjust the composition more precisely.

Adding Text Stamps (Optional): Some advanced Nikon Coolpix models might allow you to embed text stamps on your images, such as the date, time, or copyright information.

Using In-Camera Editing:

1. Playback the image you want to edit in review mode.

2. Locate the Edit button on the camera's controls. It might be a dedicated button or an option within the playback menu (consult your camera's manual for specifics).

3. Select the desired editing function from the available options, such as Trim, D-Lighting, Filter Effects, etc.

4. The camera might display further options depending on the chosen editing function. For example, with D-Lighting, you might be able to adjust the level of shadow recovery.

5. Make your adjustments and save the edited image as a new file. The original image remains unaltered.

Important Notes:

- The availability of specific in-camera editing functions might vary depending on the Nikon Coolpix P950 model and firmware version. Consult your camera's manual for a complete list of editing options.

- In-camera editing features are generally less powerful and versatile compared to dedicated photo editing software on a computer or mobile device.

- It's always recommended to keep the original unedited image for archival purposes, especially if you plan on extensive editing later.

The Nikon Coolpix P950's in-camera editing capabilities are limited, they can be helpful for making minor adjustments or quick enhancements to your photos before transferring them to your computer for more advanced editing.

CHAPTER SIX
ADVANCED FEATURES

Using the Electronic Viewfinder (EVF)

The Nikon Coolpix P950 features a high-resolution electronic viewfinder (EVF) for composing and reviewing your photos and videos. Here's a guide on using the EVF:

Activating the EVF:

1. **Turn on the camera:** Ensure your Nikon Coolpix P950 is powered on.

2. **Bring your eye to the viewfinder:** Locate the EVF eyepiece on the back of the camera, usually on the left side near the LCD screen. Lift the eyecup surrounding the eyepiece for comfort.

3. **Automatic switching (default):** In most cases, the camera will automatically switch from the LCD screen to the EVF when you bring your eye close to the viewfinder. This is due to an eye sensor located next to the eyepiece.

Checking the Auto Toggle Setting (Optional):

You can verify if the automatic EVF toggle is enabled in the camera menu:

- Access the menu by pressing the **Menu button**. (See previous steps in response "The Menu System" for locating the Menu button).

- Navigate to the **Setup** or **Settings** menu using the multi selector buttons.

- Look for an option labelled **EVF auto toggle** or similar.

- Ensure this option is set to **On** for automatic switching to the EVF when using the viewfinder.

Manual Switching (if applicable):

Some camera models might also have a dedicated button to manually toggle between the LCD and EVF. Consult your camera's manual if you have this option and want to know the button's location.

Using the EVF:

- Once you're looking through the EVF, you'll see the camera's live view feed with all the shooting information and overlays displayed according to your camera settings.

- Compose your shot and capture the image by pressing the shutter release button halfway to focus and fully down to take the picture.

- You can review captured photos or videos through the EVF as well.

Additional Notes:

- The EVF displays a high-resolution image, offering a clear view of the scene you're framing, especially helpful in bright outdoor conditions where the LCD screen might be difficult to see.
- Some settings might only be visible or adjustable through the EVF, such as exposure information or focus peaking.
- Eye sensor sensitivity can be adjusted in the camera menu on some models. This can be helpful if the camera accidentally switches between the EVF and LCD screen due to minor movements near the eye sensor.

Here's an image of a Nikon Coolpix P950 with the viewfinder highlighted:

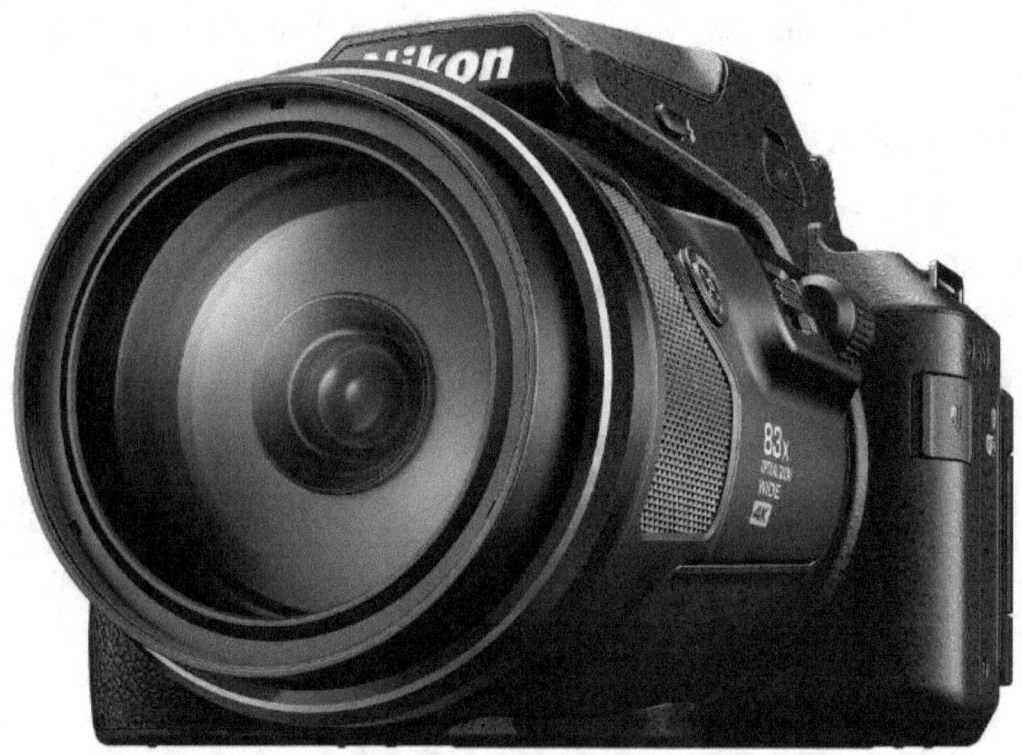

By following these steps and understanding the functionality of the EVF, you can effectively use it to compose your shots and enhance your shooting experience with the Nikon Coolpix P950.

Wi-Fi and Bluetooth Connectivity

The Nikon Coolpix P950 offers both Wi-Fi and Bluetooth connectivity, allowing you to connect your camera to your smartphone for expanded functionality.

Here's a breakdown of what you can do with each type of connection, along with an image for illustration:

Wi-Fi

- **Image Downloading:** Transfer photos and videos to your smartphone for sharing, editing, or backing up. You can choose full resolution or smaller file sizes for faster transfers.

- **Remote Shooting:** Use your smartphone as a remote control for the camera. This is helpful for capturing photos from a distance, minimizing camera shake, or getting creative angles. The Nikon SnapBridge app lets you see a live view from the camera on your phone, compose your shot, and trigger the shutter remotely.

- **Location Tagging (Optional):** If your smartphone allows location sharing, the camera can embed GPS data into your photos when connected via Wi-Fi. This helps you remember where you took a particular picture.

Bluetooth

- **Low-Energy Connection:** Bluetooth on the Coolpix P950 uses a low-power connection to maintain a constant link with your smartphone.

- **SnapBridge App Pairing:** The initial pairing between your camera and smartphone likely uses Bluetooth for setup. The Nikon SnapBridge app facilitates this process.

- **Automatic Image Download (Reduced Quality):** With Bluetooth Low Energy (BLE) enabled, the camera can automatically transfer lower-resolution versions of your captured images to your smartphone in the background. This is a convenient way to quickly share snapshots or preview images on your phone without needing a full Wi-Fi connection.

Using Wi-Fi and Bluetooth:

1. **Install the Nikon SnapBridge App:** Download and install the free Nikon SnapBridge app on your compatible smartphone (iOS or Android).

2. **Turn on Wi-Fi and Bluetooth on the Camera:** Access the camera's menu and navigate to the network settings section (consult your camera's manual for specific instructions). Enable both Wi-Fi and Bluetooth.

3. **Pair the Camera with Your Phone:** Launch the SnapBridge app on your smartphone and follow the on-screen instructions to initiate pairing with your Nikon Coolpix P950. This usually involves selecting the camera's Wi-Fi network from your phone's Wi-Fi settings and entering a password (displayed on the camera) for the initial connection.

Benefits of Using Wi-Fi and Bluetooth:

- **Wireless Image Transfer:** Share photos and videos conveniently without cables.

- **Remote Shooting:** Capture photos remotely for creative control or minimizing camera shake.

- **Location Tagging (Optional):** Geotag your photos with location information.

- **Automatic Image Preview (Bluetooth):** Get a quick preview of your photos on your phone without a full Wi-Fi connection.

Things to Remember:

- Ensure your smartphone is compatible with the Nikon SnapBridge app.

- The initial connection setup might involve both Wi-Fi and Bluetooth.

- For full-resolution image downloads and advanced remote shooting features, a Wi-Fi connection is recommended.

- Bluetooth Low Energy provides a constant connection for automatic background image transfers (reduced quality) and consumes less battery power compared to Wi-Fi.

By utilizing Wi-Fi and Bluetooth connectivity with the Nikon SnapBridge app, you can enhance your photography experience with the Nikon Coolpix P950 by transferring photos wirelessly, exploring remote shooting options, and sharing your creativity on the go.

Shooting in RAW format

The Nikon Coolpix P950 allows you to capture images in RAW format, along with the standard JPEG format. Here's a breakdown of RAW photography and how to enable it on your Coolpix P950, along with an image for reference:

What is RAW Format?

- RAW format, sometimes referred to as "digital negative," captures all the data from the camera's sensor at the time the picture is taken.

- Unlike JPEG, which compresses the image file for smaller storage size, RAW files are uncompressed and retain all the detail and information from the sensor.

Benefits of Shooting in RAW:

- **Greater Image Quality:** RAW files offer more detail, dynamic range (the range of light and dark tones in a photo), and flexibility for editing compared to JPEGs.

- **More Control in Post-Processing:** RAW files allow for more extensive editing in software like Adobe Lightroom or Photoshop. You can adjust white balance, exposure, shadows, highlights, and other aspects of the image with greater precision without sacrificing quality.

Drawbacks of Shooting in RAW:

- **Larger File Sizes:** RAW files are significantly larger than JPEGs, requiring more storage space on your memory card.

- **Requires Post-Processing:** RAW files need to be processed into a viewable format (like JPEG or TIFF) using editing software before you can share them easily.

How to Shoot in RAW on Nikon Coolpix P950:

1. **Access the Menu:** Press the **Menu button**(usually labeled with the word "Menu" or lines) on the back of the camera.

2. **Navigate to the Shooting Menu:** Use the multi selector buttons (the four-directional buttons on the back) to navigate through the tabs or menus. Look for a tab labelled **Shooting Menu**, **Settings**, or similar and press the multi selector right button to enter.

3. **Find the Image Quality Setting:** Scroll through the menu options using the up/down buttons of the multi selector. Look for an option labelled **Image Quality**, **Image Size/Quality**, or similar. Press the multi selector right button to enter this submenu.

4. **Select RAW Image Format:** Within the Image Quality submenu, you'll see options for image size and file format. There might be a selection for **Fine** or **Normal** JPEG quality, and an option for **RAW**. Choose the **RAW** option (or RAW + JPEG if you want both RAW and a smaller JPEG copy).

5. **Exit the Menu:** Press the **Menu button** repeatedly to exit the sub-menus and return to the shooting screen.

Shooting with RAW Enabled:

- Once you've enabled RAW shooting, the camera will capture images in RAW format. You'll notice the file format indicator on the camera's LCD screen might change to reflect RAW capture.

Additional Notes:

- Consult your camera's manual for specific instructions and menu navigation details, as the wording of menu options might vary slightly depending on the model and firmware version.

- Consider the extra storage space requirements when shooting in RAW format. Invest in a high-capacity memory card if you plan to use RAW extensively.

- If you're new to RAW photography, you might need to learn about RAW image processing software to unlock the full potential of RAW files.

By understanding RAW format and enabling it on your Nikon Coolpix P950, you can capture images with more detail and flexibility for creating stunning photos through post-processing editing.

Customizing Buttons and Menus

The Nikon Coolpix P950 offers limited customization options for buttons and menus compared to some higher-end Nikon DSLRs or mirrorless cameras. However, there are still some ways to personalize your shooting experience:

Function (Fn) Button:

- The Fn button, usually located near the shutter release button, can be programmed to access a specific function quickly.
- By default, it might be set to functions like Continuous Shooting mode.
- Access the camera menu and navigate to the settings related to the Fn button (consult your camera's manual for specific menu locations). You can choose from a list of functions to assign to the Fn button based on your preferences.

My Menu (Optional):

- Some Nikon Coolpix models might offer a "My Menu" feature. This allows you to create a personalized menu with frequently used settings for quick access.
- Explore your camera's menu system to see if a "My Menu" option is available. If so, you can add or remove functions from this menu to suit your shooting style.

Review Mode Playback Display:

- You can customize the information displayed when reviewing captured photos during playback.
- In playback mode, press the info button (usually a button with a circled "i") to cycle through different information overlays on the screen, such as histogram, exposure information, or shooting mode.

Custom Picture Controls (Optional):

- While not directly related to button customization, Nikon Coolpix P950 offers Creative Picture Controls that provide various color and image processing effects. You can customize these picture controls to create your own presets for specific shooting scenarios.

General Tips:

- Familiarize yourself with the camera's default functions and button placements. This will help you determine which functions you might want quicker access to through customization.

- Read your camera's manual for detailed instructions on accessing and customizing the Fn button, My Menu (if available), and Review mode playback display options.

- Experiment with different settings and button assignments to find a setup that works best for your shooting style.

Remember:

- The Coolpix P950's customization options are more limited than high-end cameras.

- Focus on personalizing the Fn button and reviewing the available menu options for the most significant impact on your shooting experience.

By exploring these customization options, you can personalize your Nikon Coolpix P950 to a certain extent and optimize your shooting workflow.

CHAPTER SEVEN
ACCESSSORIES

Tripods

A tripod is an essential accessory for any photographer using the Nikon Coolpix P950, especially considering its impressive 83x zoom. It provides stability and reduces camera shake, resulting in sharper images, especially at slower shutter speeds and high zoom ranges. Here are some factors to consider when choosing a tripod for your Nikon Coolpix P950:

Types of Tripods:

- **Tripod Material:** Tripods are commonly made from aluminium or carbon fibre. Aluminium tripods are generally more affordable but heavier. Carbon fibre tripods are lighter and more portable but tend to be more expensive.

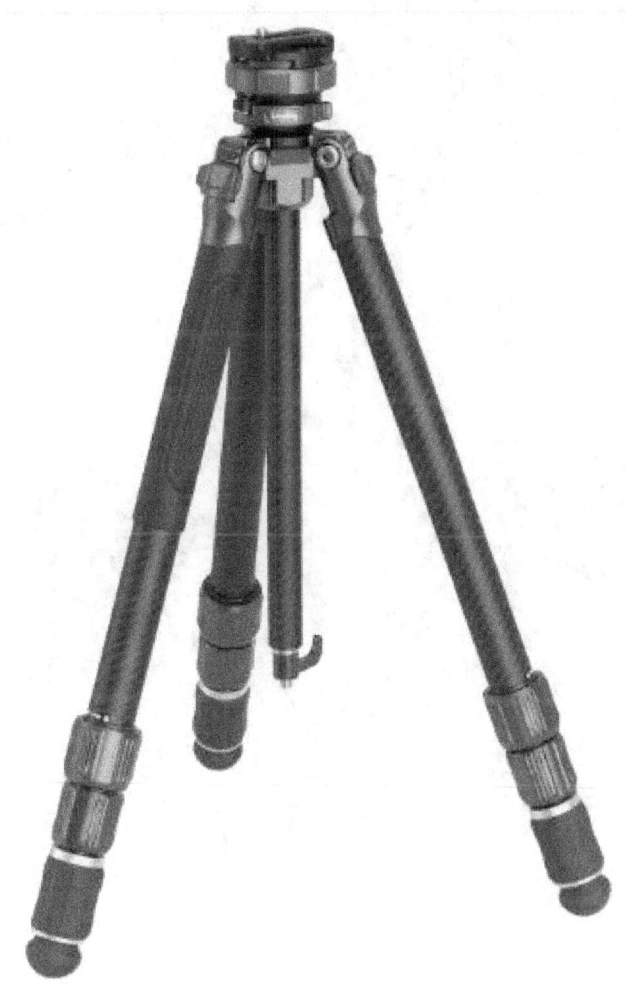

- **Height:** Consider the height you need. Ideally, the tripod should allow you to comfortably frame your shots while standing upright. Look for tripods with adjustable legs and a centre column that extends for additional height.

- **Weight Capacity:** The tripod should be able to support the weight of your Nikon Coolpix P950 with a lens attached, plus any additional accessories you might use.

- **Head Type:** Most tripods come with a tripod head that allows you to pan (move horizontally) and tilt (move vertically) the camera for composing your shots. There are various tripod head types, including ball heads, pan-tilt heads, and fluid heads. A ball head is a good option for the Nikon Coolpix P950, offering good versatility and ease of use.

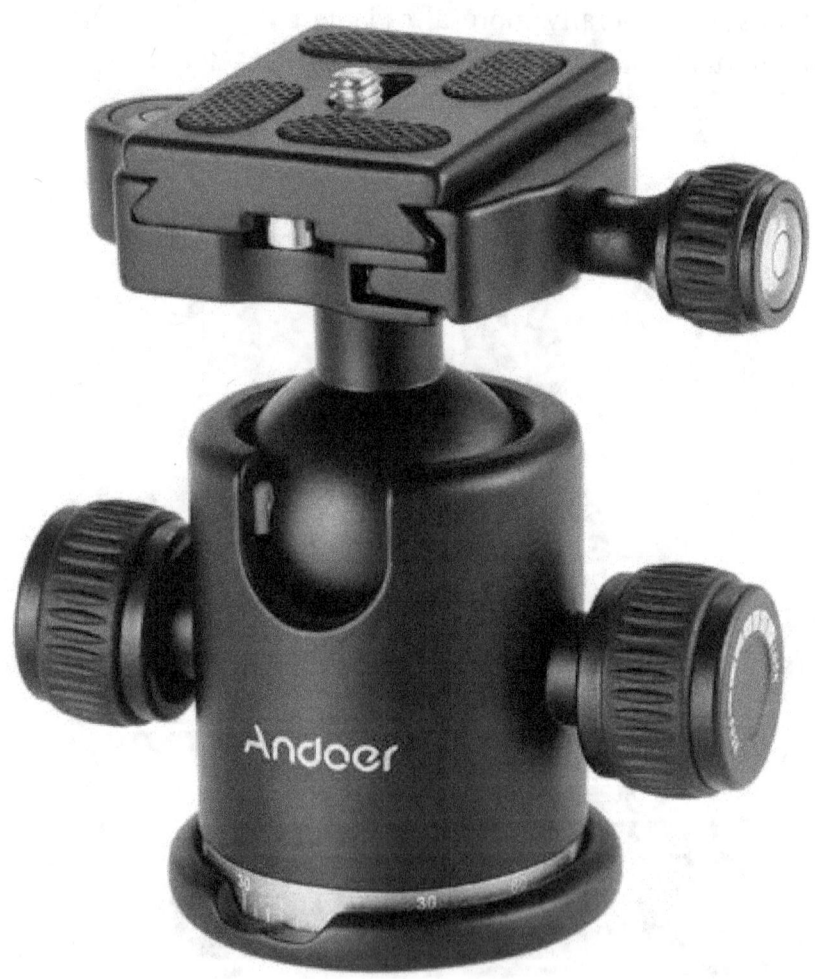

Additional Features:

- **Leg Locks:** Look for tripods with flip locks or twist locks for easy and secure leg adjustments.

- **Rubber Feet:** Rubber feet provide stability and prevent the tripod from slipping on smooth surfaces.
- **Carrying Case:** A carrying case is helpful for protecting and transporting your tripod.

Here are some specific tripod recommendations for the Nikon Coolpix P950:

- **Joby GorillaPod 1K Stand:** This compact and portable tripod is a great option for travel or everyday use. It features flexible legs that can wrap around objects for creative shot possibilities. It can support up to 1.1 pounds (0.5 kg), which is sufficient for the Coolpix P950.

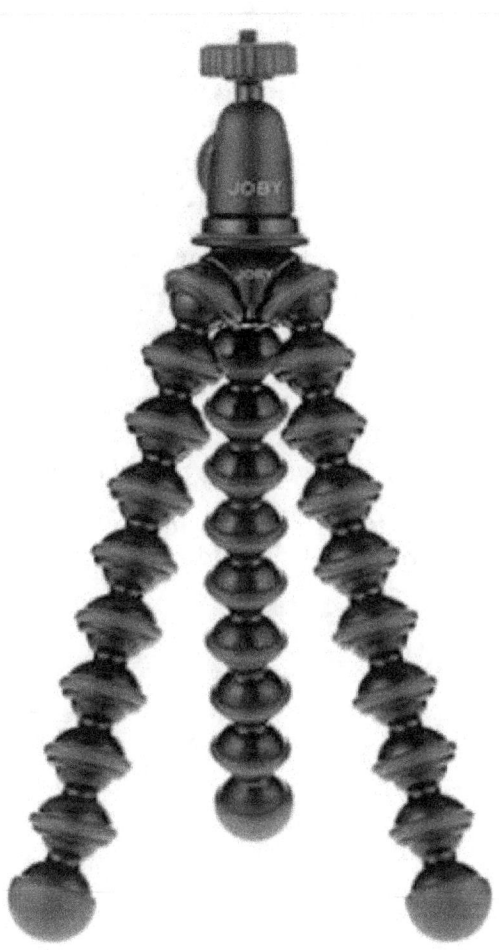

- **Manfrotto PIXI Mini Tripod:** Another compact and lightweight tripod option, the Manfrotto PIXI is perfect for travel and everyday use. It can support up to 3.3 pounds (1.5 kg), making it suitable for the Coolpix P950 and even a small mirrorless camera.

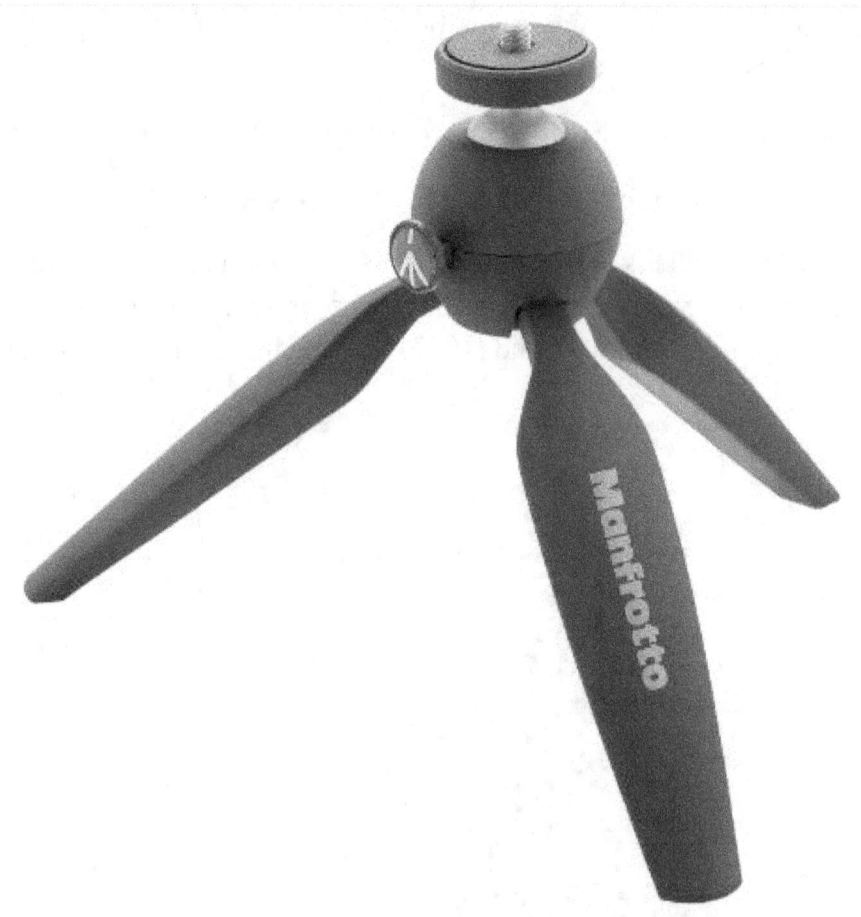

- **Mefoto RoadTrip Travel Tripod:** This versatile tripod offers a good balance of portability, stability, and affordability. It extends to a good height and can support up to 8.8 pounds (4 kg), making it suitable for the Coolpix P950 and even a full-frame DSLR camera.

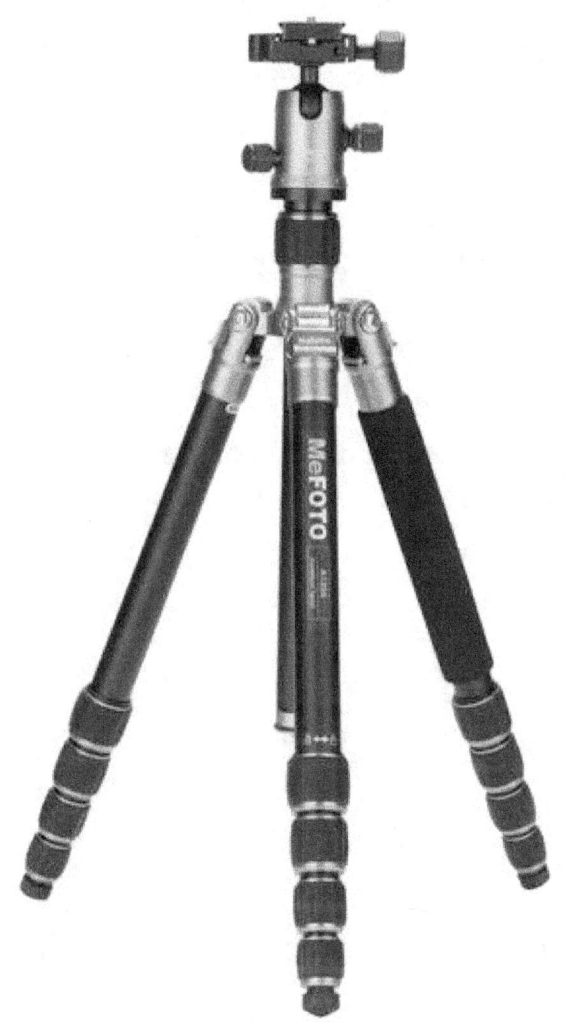

The best tripod for you depends on your individual needs and budget. Consider the factors mentioned above and try out different tripods if possible, to find one that feels comfortable and sturdy for you and your Nikon Coolpix P950.

External Flashes

The Nikon Coolpix P950 doesn't support dedicated external flashes in the traditional sense. Unlike DSLRs or mirrorless cameras with a hot shoe that provides a connection point for external flashes with high voltage triggers, the Coolpix P950's hot shoe is designed for a different purpose.

Here's what you need to know about using external flashes with the Nikon Coolpix P950:

Compatibility:

- **Nikon CLS System Flashes Not Compatible:** Standard Nikon external flashes with the Nikon Creative Lighting System (CLS) are not compatible with the Coolpix P950. Their high voltage trigger systems could damage the camera's internal circuitry.

Alternative Solutions:

- **Speedlights with Wireless Optical Masters:** While the Coolpix P950 doesn't have a standard hot shoe for direct flash connection, you can explore alternative flash options. Consider using speedlights (external flashes) that have built-in wireless optical triggering capabilities. These flashes can communicate with the camera's built-in flash and fire remotely.

- **Manual Flashes:** You can also use manual flashes that don't rely on complex triggering systems. These flashes would require manual power adjustments and wouldn't offer features like automatic flash exposure.

Using the Built-in Flash:

- The Coolpix P950's built-in flash can be a helpful solution for basic fill lighting in low-light situations. It can be bounced off a ceiling or wall for softer lighting.

- Explore the camera's flash modes (auto, red-eye reduction, etc.) to find the best setting for your needs.

Things to Consider When Using External Flashes:

- **Line of Sight:** Since you'll be relying on the camera's built-in flash to trigger the remote flash wirelessly, there needs to be a clear line of sight between the two units for proper communication.

- **Manual Power Adjustments:** With some remote flash setups, you might need to adjust the flash power manually on the flash unit itself.

The Nikon Coolpix P950 doesn't support traditional Nikon external flashes, there are alternative solutions using wireless optical flashes or manual flashes for those who need more lighting control than the built-in flash offers. Keep in mind the limitations and additional considerations when using these external flash options.

Remote Controls

The Nikon Coolpix P950 offers two main options for remote control:

1. Wireless Remote Control (Nikon ML-L7):

- This is the official remote control offered by Nikon specifically designed for the Coolpix P950 and other compatible Nikon cameras. It connects wirelessly via Bluetooth for a cable-free shooting experience.

- The Nikon ML-L7 features a dedicated shutter release button for capturing photos remotely. This is useful for situations where you want to minimize camera shake, such as in low-light conditions or when using slow shutter speeds.

- Some models might also have a zoom control button for operating the zoom remotely. However, functionality might vary depending on the specific version of the ML-L7 you purchase. Double-check the features listed on the product description before buying.

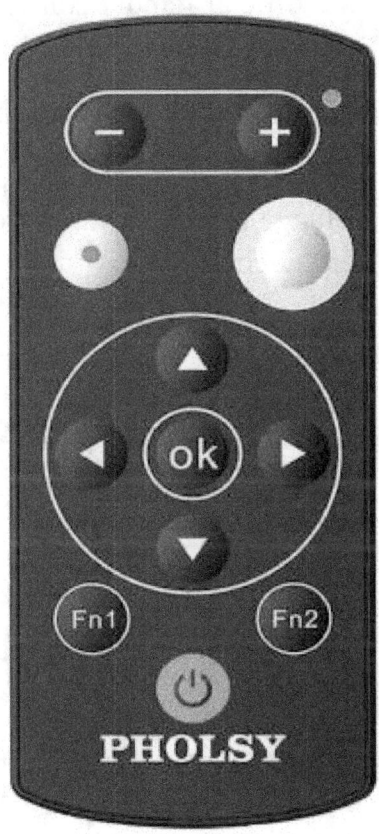
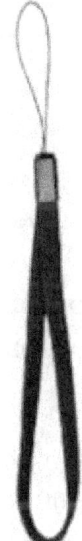

2. Third-Party Wireless Remote Controls:

- Several third-party manufacturers offer wireless remote controls compatible with the Nikon Coolpix P950 through Bluetooth or infrared (IR) technology.

- These remotes may offer similar functionality to the Nikon ML-L7, including a shutter release button and potentially zoom controls. They may also have additional features like intervalometer functions for time-lapse photography or video record start/stop buttons.

- When considering third-party options, ensure compatibility with the Coolpix P950 and Bluetooth connectivity for reliable remote control.

Here's a breakdown of some factors to consider when choosing a remote control for your Nikon Coolpix P905:

- **Brand and Model:** The Nikon ML-L7 is the official remote control, but explore third-party options if you need specific features or a more budget-friendly solution.

- **Functionality:** Consider the buttons and features you need, such as a shutter release button, zoom control, and any additional functionalities offered by some third-party remotes.

- **Range:** While most remotes offer a decent range (often 10 meters or more), check the specifications for the specific model you're considering.

- **Battery Life:** Remote controls typically use small coin batteries. The battery life can vary depending on usage.

Using a Remote Control:

- **Pairing:** Both the Nikon ML-L7 and most third-party remote controls require pairing with your camera for the first time. Refer to the manual of your specific remote for pairing instructions. The process usually involves enabling Bluetooth on the camera and following the remote's instructions for pairing.

- **Operation:** Once paired, you can use the remote control's buttons to trigger the shutter release, zoom the lens (if supported), and potentially control other camera functions depending on the model.

Benefits of Using a Remote Control:

- **Minimizing Camera Shake:** Using a remote control eliminates the need to touch the camera, which can introduce camera shake and blur images, especially in low-light or slow shutter speed situations.

- **Creative Shooting:** A remote control allows you to trigger the shutter from a distance, helpful for capturing wildlife, self-portraits, or group photos where you want to be in the picture.

- **Convenience:** A remote control offers convenience, especially when the camera is mounted on a tripod or in a difficult-to-reach location.

By considering these factors and your shooting needs, you can choose the most suitable remote control to enhance your experience with the Nikon Coolpix P950.

Carrying Cases

There are various carrying case options available for the Nikon Coolpix P950, ranging from compact pouches to backpacks designed for camera gear. Here are some factors to consider when choosing a carrying case:

- **Size and Weight:** The size and weight of the case should depend on how much you plan to carry. A compact pouch might be sufficient if you only carry the camera itself. Opt for a backpack if you plan to carry additional accessories like lenses, extra batteries, or a tripod.

- **Protection:** The case should provide adequate padding to protect your camera from bumps, scratches, and dust. Consider cases with padded dividers to keep your camera separate from other gear.

- **Style:** Carrying cases come in various styles, from backpacks and sling bags to hard-shell cases. Choose a style that suits your personal preference and carrying needs.

Here are some specific carrying case recommendations for the Nikon Coolpix P950:

- **Compact Camera Pouch:** This is a good option for minimalists who just want to carry the camera itself. These pouches are lightweight and easy to slip into a backpack or purse.

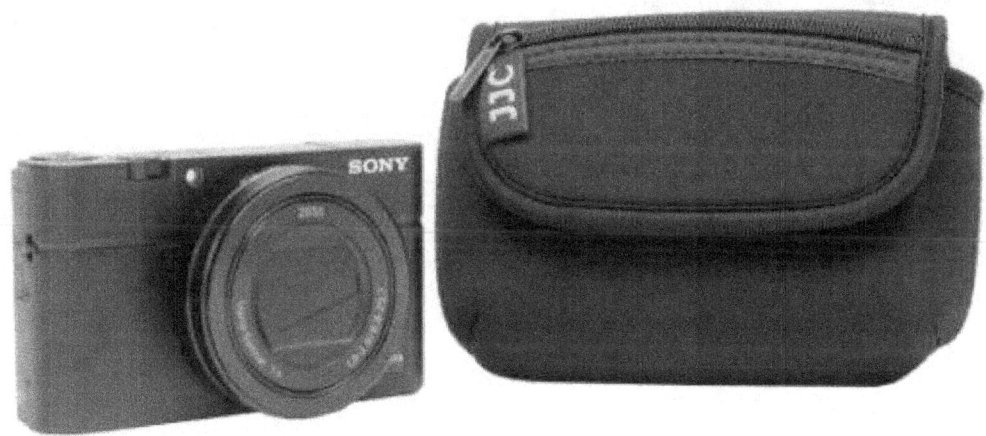

- **Camera Sling Bag:** A sling bag offers a comfortable way to carry your camera and some essential accessories. It provides easy access to your gear while keeping it protected.

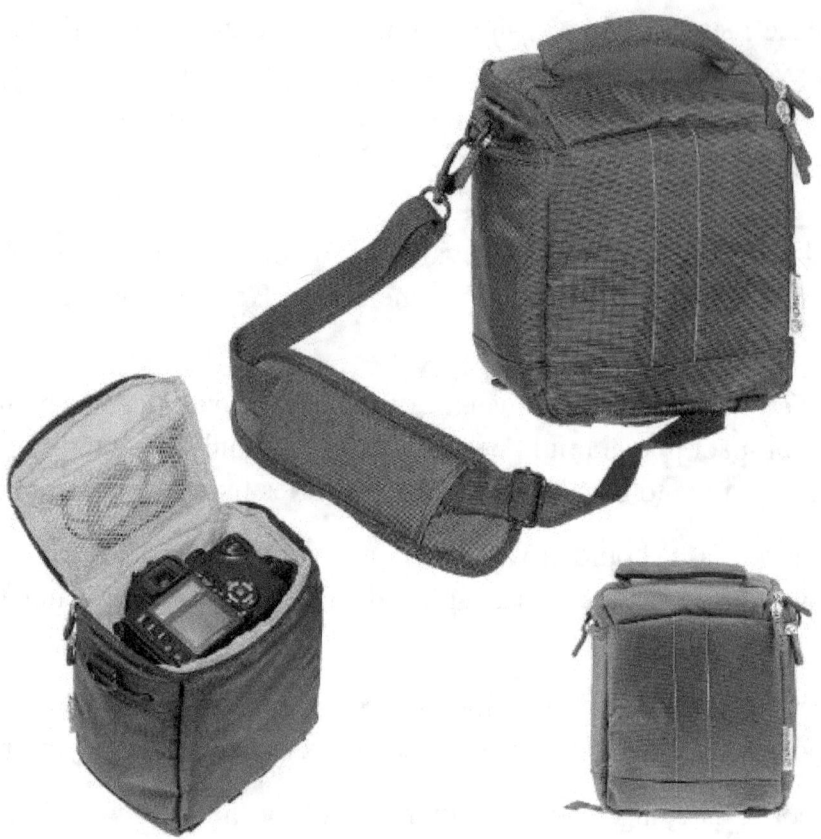

- **Camera Backpack:** A backpack is ideal for photographers who carry a lot of gear, such as extra lenses, batteries, a tripod, and other accessories. Backpacks distribute the weight evenly, making them comfortable for carrying for longer periods.

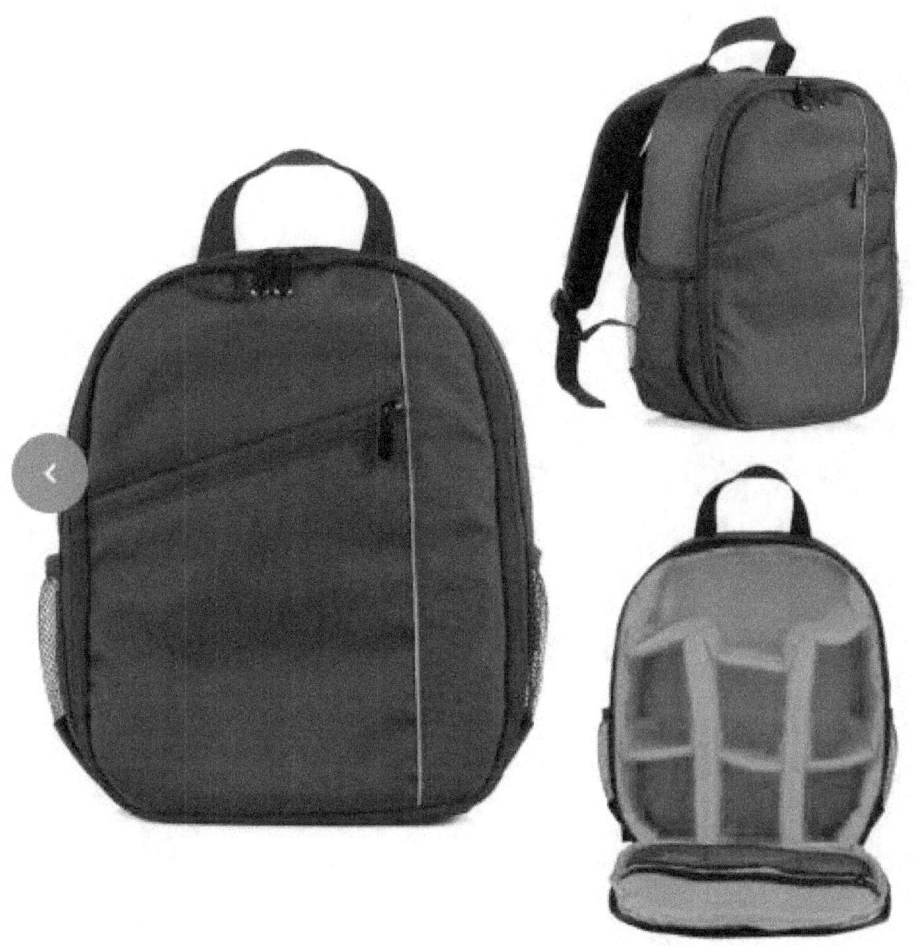

Additional Tips:

- **Consider weather resistance:** If you plan to shoot in wet or dusty conditions, look for a case with weather-resistant materials.

- **Think about future needs:** If you plan to expand your camera gear in the future, choose a case that can accommodate your growing equipment collection.

By considering these factors and your shooting style, you can choose the perfect carrying case to protect your Nikon Coolpix P950 and keep it organized while you're on the go.

CHAPTER EIGHT
TROUBLESHOOTING

Common Camera Problems

The Nikon Coolpix P950, like any camera, can encounter some occasional issues. Here are some common problems you might face and some troubleshooting tips:

Image Quality Issues:

- **Blurry Images:** This can be caused by camera shake, especially at high zoom ranges. Use a tripod for better stability. Also, ensure the subject and lens are in focus.

- **Images Appear Too Bright or Dark:** This is related to exposure. Try adjusting exposure compensation settings or using different shooting modes.

- **Grainy Images (Noise):** Appears in low-light photos due to high ISO settings. Experiment with lower ISOs and using a flash if possible.

Focusing Problems:

- **Camera Won't Focus:** Make sure the subject is within the minimum focusing distance of the lens. Clean the lens for any obstructions. Switch to manual focus mode and adjust the focus ring to achieve sharpness.

Battery Issues:

- **Battery Drains Quickly:** Using features like the zoom frequently, Wi-Fi, or the EVF can drain the battery faster. Turn off these features when not in use. Carry a spare battery for extended shooting sessions.

Error Messages:

- **Lens Error:** Turn the camera off and on again. If the error persists, remove and reattach the lens. Dirty lens contacts might be an issue. If none of these work, consult a professional.

- **Memory Card Error:** Ensure the card is inserted correctly and formatted for the camera. Try a different memory card.

Other Issues:

- **Camera Won't Turn On:** Make sure the battery is charged and properly inserted. Check for any damage to the power button.

- **LCD Screen Not Working:** If the screen is dirty, clean it gently with a microfiber cloth. If it's damaged, it might require professional repair.

General Tips:

- **Consult the camera manual:** It provides detailed instructions for troubleshooting common problems.
- **Keep the camera firmware updated:** Updates can fix bugs and improve performance.
- **Use a camera bag:** Protect your camera from bumps, scratches, and dust.

By understanding these common problems and following these tips, you can keep your Nikon Coolpix P950 functioning smoothly and capture amazing photos for years to come.

Error Messages

The Nikon Coolpix P950 displays specific error messages to indicate when something isn't working as expected. Here's a breakdown of some common error messages and troubleshooting steps:

Memory Card Errors:

- "Memory card error" or "Card cannot be used"
- "Card is write-protected"

These messages typically point to issues with the memory card itself. Try the following:

- **Turn the camera off and on again.** A simple restart can sometimes resolve temporary glitches.
- **Ensure the card is inserted correctly.** Make sure it's fully inserted in the designated slot and oriented properly.
- **Check the write protect switch.** Some SD cards have a physical switch to prevent accidental data deletion. If enabled (usually a slide switch on the side), flip it to the unlocked position.
- **Format the card in the camera.** Formatting erases all data, so back up important photos beforehand. Formatting creates a file system compatible with the camera, potentially resolving errors.
- **Try a different memory card.** If the issue persists with one card, another card might be faulty. Use cards recommended by Nikon for optimal performance and compatibility.

Battery Errors:

- "Battery low"

This is a straightforward message indicating the battery needs replacing.

- "Cannot recharge battery"

This message suggests an issue with the battery or charger. Here's what you can try:

- **Use a different battery.** If you have a spare charged battery, try using that to see if the camera functions normally.
- **Ensure the battery is inserted correctly.** Make sure the battery contacts are clean and free of corrosion.
- **Use the original Nikon charger.** Third-party chargers might not always be compatible or function optimally.

Lens Errors:

- **"An error occurred in lens operation"**

This message might indicate the lens is stuck or obstructed.

- **Turn the camera off and on again.** A restart can sometimes resolve minor lens issues.
- **Avoid forcing the lens.** If the lens is jammed, don't try to force it. Gently try moving the zoom rocker in both directions.
- **Clean the lens contacts.** Dust or debris on the lens contacts can prevent proper communication between the lens and camera body. Use a blower or cotton swab to gently clean the contacts.
- **If none of these solutions work, consult a Nikon authorized service centre.**

Other Errors:

- **"System error"**

This is a generic error message indicating a more complex issue within the camera.

- **Turn the camera off and on again.** A restart can sometimes resolve temporary glitches.
- **Update the camera firmware.** Newer firmware can fix bugs and improve camera performance. Check the Nikon website for updates and follow the instructions for installation.
- **If the error persists, contact Nikon support or a service centre.** They can provide further diagnosis and repair options.

Remember: For detailed troubleshooting steps specific to your error message, refer to the Nikon Coolpix P950 manual. It provides comprehensive information and illustrations to guide you through the process.

Cleaning and Maintenance Tips

The Nikon Coolpix P950 is a powerful camera, but like any electronic device, it requires proper care to ensure optimal performance and longevity. Here are some cleaning and maintenance tips to keep your P950 functioning smoothly:

Lens Care:

- The lens is the most delicate part of your camera. Avoid touching the lens glass with your fingers.

- Use a blower or a soft lens brush to gently remove dust particles from the lens surface.

- If fingerprints or smudges are present, use a microfiber cleaning cloth specifically designed for lenses. Wipe gently in circular motions from the centre outwards. Avoid using abrasive cloths or cleaning solutions that can damage the lens coating.

- To clean the front lens element (the outermost part), you can moisten the microfiber cloth with a lens cleaning solution or distilled water. Wring out any excess moisture before wiping the lens.

- Never use solvents, alcohol, or harsh chemicals on the lens, as they can damage the coating.

- When not in use, keep the lens covered with the lens cap to protect it from dust, scratches, and fingerprints.

Sensor Cleaning:

- The sensor is extremely sensitive and prone to dust spots appearing in images. It's generally recommended to leave sensor cleaning to professional services unless you're comfortable with the process.

- If you notice dust spots, you can try using the camera's built-in sensor cleaning function (if available). Consult the manual for specific instructions on how to activate it.

- Avoid using manual sensor cleaning swabs unless absolutely necessary, as improper cleaning can damage the sensor.

Body Cleaning:

- Use a soft, dry microfiber cloth to wipe down the camera body.

- For stubborn dirt or grime, you can slightly dampen the cloth with distilled water. Wring out any excess moisture before wiping the camera.

- Avoid using abrasive cleaners, solvents, or alcohol, as they can damage the camera's finish.

General Maintenance:

- Store your camera in a cool, dry place away from direct sunlight and extreme temperatures.
- Avoid exposing the camera to sudden changes in temperature or humidity, as this can cause condensation and potentially damage internal components.
- Remove the battery and SD card when the camera is not in use for extended periods.
- It's recommended to periodically turn on the camera and take a few test shots to keep the internal mechanisms functioning properly.
- Update the camera firmware whenever new updates are available. Newer firmware can improve performance and fix bugs.

Additional Tips:

- Invest in a camera bag to protect your P950 from bumps, scratches, and dust during transport.
- Avoid touching the camera with wet or greasy hands.
- Be mindful of where you place the camera. Avoid setting it down on dirty or sandy surfaces.

By following these cleaning and maintenance tips, you can ensure your Nikon Coolpix P950 captures stunning images for years to come. If you have any concerns or if dust becomes a persistent problem, consult a professional camera service centre for cleaning.

Firmware Updates

Keeping your Nikon Coolpix P950's firmware up-to-date ensures you have the latest features, bug fixes, and performance improvements. Here's a breakdown of the update process:

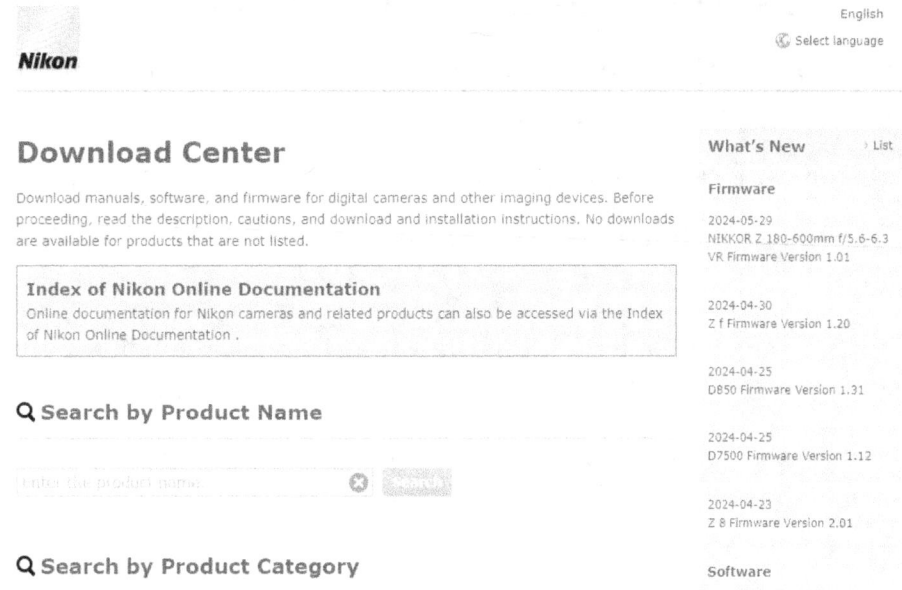

Checking for Updates:

- The first step is to verify if a newer firmware version is available for your P950.
- Visit the Nikon Download Centre
- Select your region and then search for "Coolpix P950."
- The download page will list available downloads, including firmware updates. It will also mention the improvements or fixes addressed in the update.

Downloading the Firmware:

- If a newer version is available, click the "Download" button next to the firmware update.
- Save the downloaded file to a location on your computer that you can easily access.

Preparing the Camera:

- **Format an SD card:** Ensure the SD card you'll be using is formatted in the camera itself. Formatting erases all data on the card, so back up any important photos or videos beforehand.
- **Charge the battery:** It's recommended to have a fully charged battery in the camera during the update process.

Transferring the Firmware to the Camera (Two Methods):

Method 1: Using an SD Card:

1. **Extract the downloaded firmware file:** Most downloaded files will be compressed. Extract the folder containing the actual firmware file (.bin file).
2. **Copy the firmware file:** Copy the extracted firmware file (usually named "firmware.bin") to the root directory of your formatted SD card.
3. **Turn off the camera:** Ensure the camera is powered off completely.
4. **Insert the SD card:** Insert the SD card containing the firmware file into the camera's SD card slot.
5. **Turn on the camera while holding the Fn button:** While holding the Fn button on the back of the camera, turn the camera on using the power button.
6. **Follow the on-screen instructions:** The camera will display a confirmation message about the update. Follow any on-screen prompts to proceed with the update.

7. **Do not turn off the camera:** During the update process, a progress bar might be displayed. It's crucial not to turn off the camera or remove the SD card until the update is complete.

8. **Camera restarts:** Once the update is finished, the camera will automatically restart.

Method 2: Using a Computer (For Windows Users Only):

- **Download the Nikon Software Updater:** You might need additional software to update the firmware using a computer. Download the Nikon Software Updater compatible with your operating system from the Nikon Download Centre.

- **Install the Updater:** Follow the on-screen instructions to install the Nikon Software Updater on your computer.

- **Connect the camera to your computer:** Use a USB cable to connect your camera to your computer. Ensure the camera is turned on.

- **Launch the Updater:** Open the Nikon Software Updater program on your computer.

- **Follow the on-screen instructions:** The Updater software will detect your camera and guide you through the update process. This might involve steps like selecting the downloaded firmware file and confirming the update.

Verifying the Update:

- Once the update is complete, turn off the camera and remove the SD card (if used).

- Turn the camera back on.

- Access the camera's menu system and navigate to the "Setup" or "Firmware" section (refer to your camera manual for specific instructions).

- The menu should display the current firmware version. Verify that it matches the version you downloaded and installed.

Important Notes:

- **Follow the instructions carefully:** It's crucial to follow the instructions provided by Nikon for your specific camera model and chosen update method (SD card or computer) to avoid any issues.

- **Only use genuine Nikon batteries:** Using a third-party battery with a low charge could potentially interrupt the update process and damage your camera.

- **Avoid interruptions:** Do not turn off the camera, remove the battery or SD card, or disconnect the USB cable during the update.

By following these steps and precautions, you can successfully update your Nikon Coolpix P950's firmware and ensure it operates at its best.

CHAPTER NINE
APPENDIX

Specifications

Here's a table summarizing the key specifications of the Nikon Coolpix P950:

Feature	Specification
Image Sensor	1/2.3-inch CMOS sensor
Effective Pixels (approx.)	16.0 million
Lens	NIKKOR lens with 83x optical zoom, 166x Dynamic Fine Zoom
Focal Length (35mm format equivalent)	24mm - 2000mm
Maximum Aperture	f/2.8 (Wide) - f/6.5 (Telephoto)
Image Stabilization	Dual Detect Optical VR (Vibration Reduction)
Autofocus System	Contrast-detect AF
Viewfinder	Electronic viewfinder (EVF) with approx. 2359k dots
Monitor	3.2-inch vari-angle TFT LCD touchscreen with approx. 921k dots
Shutter Speed	1/6000 sec. to 30 sec. (Bulb)
ISO Sensitivity	100 - 6400
Metering Method	Matrix, Center-weighted, Spot
Exposure Modes	Programmed Auto (P), Shutter-Priority Auto (S), Aperture-Priority Auto (A), Manual (M)
Movie Recording	Up to 4K UHD (3840 x 2160) at 30p, Full HD (1920 x 1080) at 60p
Media	SD, SDHC, SDXC memory cards
Connectivity	Wi-Fi, Bluetooth
Battery	EN-EL20a Rechargeable Lithium-Ion Battery
Dimensions (WxHxD)	5.5 x 4.3 x 5.9 in. (139.5 x 109.6 x 181.9 mm)

| Weight (approx.) | 1005g (2 lbs 3.5 oz) (body only) |

Additional Notes

- Macro shooting distance: approx. 1 cm (0.39 in.) from the centre of the front surface of the lens
- Built-in flash with range of approx. 0.5 to 11.5 meters (1 ft. 8 in. to 37 ft.)
- Hot shoe for attaching external flashes
- Tripod socket

This table provides a quick overview of the P950's capabilities. For a more comprehensive list of specifications and detailed descriptions, you can refer to the Nikon Coolpix P950 user manual or the Nikon website.

Warranty Information

Nikon offers a standard one-year limited warranty on the Nikon Coolpix P950, similar to most of their new cameras, lenses, flashes, and accessories purchased from authorized Nikon Dealers. Here's a breakdown of what the warranty typically covers:

Warranty Coverage:

- Nikon guarantees the P950 to be free from defects in material and workmanship for one year from the original date of purchase.

What's Covered:

- Repairs to replace defective parts with new or refurbished parts at Nikon's discretion.
- Labor costs associated with these repairs.

What's Not Covered:

- Damage caused by misuse, neglect, unauthorized modification, or improper storage.
- Normal wear and tear.
- Cosmetic damage.
- Damage caused by accidents, water, sand, or other foreign objects.
- Damage caused by using unauthorized batteries, chargers, or other accessories.
- Costs of transportation, shipping, or insurance when sending the camera for repair.

How to Make a Warranty Claim:

- To make a warranty claim, you'll need the following:
    - The original dated proof of purchase (receipt) showing the product name, dealer's name, and purchase date.
    - The Nikon Coolpix P950 camera with any attached accessories experiencing the issue.
- You can contact Nikon support through their website or phone number to initiate the warranty claim process. They will provide instructions on where to send the camera for repair.

Warranty Variations:

- **Region Specific:** Warranty terms might vary slightly depending on your region. Nikon's website should have specific warranty information for your country.
- **Extended Warranties:** Nikon or authorized retailers might offer extended warranty plans that provide coverage beyond the standard one-year warranty for an additional cost.

Recommendations:

- Keep your original receipt in a safe place for warranty purposes.
- Register your camera with Nikon (usually online) for faster warranty service and to receive updates or important notifications.
- Read the full Nikon warranty document for detailed information on coverage, exclusions, and claim procedures. You can find it on the Nikon website or within the camera's user manual.

By understanding the warranty information, you'll know what to expect if you encounter any issues with your Nikon Coolpix P950 within the warranty period.

Glossary of Terms

Here's a glossary of terms you might encounter while using your Nikon Coolpix P950:

Basic Photography Terms:

- **Aperture:** The opening in the lens that controls the amount of light reaching the sensor. A wider aperture (lower f-number) lets in more light, blurring the background (shallow depth of field). A narrower aperture (higher f-number) lets in less light, creating a sharper image throughout (deep depth of field).

- **ISO:** Controls the sensor's sensitivity to light. Higher ISO allows you to shoot in low light but can introduce noise (grain) in the image.
- **Shutter Speed:** The length of time the shutter stays open, affecting how motion is captured. A faster shutter speed freezes action, while a slower shutter speed can blur motion or create light trails.
- **Zoom:** The ability of the lens to magnify a subject, bringing it closer in the frame. The Nikon Coolpix P950 boasts an impressive 83x optical zoom.
- **Focus:** Sharpening the image on a specific subject.
- **Exposure:** The combination of aperture, shutter speed, and ISO that determines the overall brightness of an image.

Camera Features:

- **Megapixels (MP):** The number of megapixels (millions of pixels) on the image sensor determines the image resolution and how much detail it can capture. The Nikon Coolpix P950 has a 16-megapixel sensor.
- **CMOS sensor:** A type of image sensor commonly used in digital cameras, known for its good low-light performance and image quality.
- **Optical Zoom:** Zoom achieved by the physical movement of lenses within the camera, resulting in high-quality magnification.
- **Dynamic Fine Zoom:** A digital zoom technology that extends the zoom range beyond the optical zoom. Image quality might be reduced at high digital zoom levels.
- **EVF (Electronic Viewfinder):** A digital viewfinder that displays an electronic image of the scene you're composing.
- **LCD Screen:** A liquid crystal display screen on the back of the camera for composing shots, reviewing images, and navigating menus.
- **Vari-angle LCD:** An LCD screen that can be tilted or swiveled for composing shots from different angles.
- **Wi-Fi:** Allows wireless image sharing and remote camera control from a smartphone or tablet.
- **Bluetooth:** Enables low-energy connections for image sharing or remote control with compatible devices.

Other:

- **Macro Mode:** A mode for capturing close-up shots of small subjects.

- **Image Stabilization:** Technology that helps reduce camera shake and blur in images.
- **Hot Shoe:** A mount on top of the camera for attaching external flashes for additional lighting.
- **Tripod Mount:** A socket on the bottom of the camera for attaching it to a tripod for stability.

By understanding these terms, you'll be able to navigate the menus, settings, and features of your Nikon Coolpix P950 with more confidence and capture stunning images.

Contacting Nikon Support

Here are the ways you can contact Nikon Support for your Nikon Coolpix P950:

Website:

- Visit the Nikon website for your region. You can find the specific URL by searching for "Nikon Support" followed by your country/region.

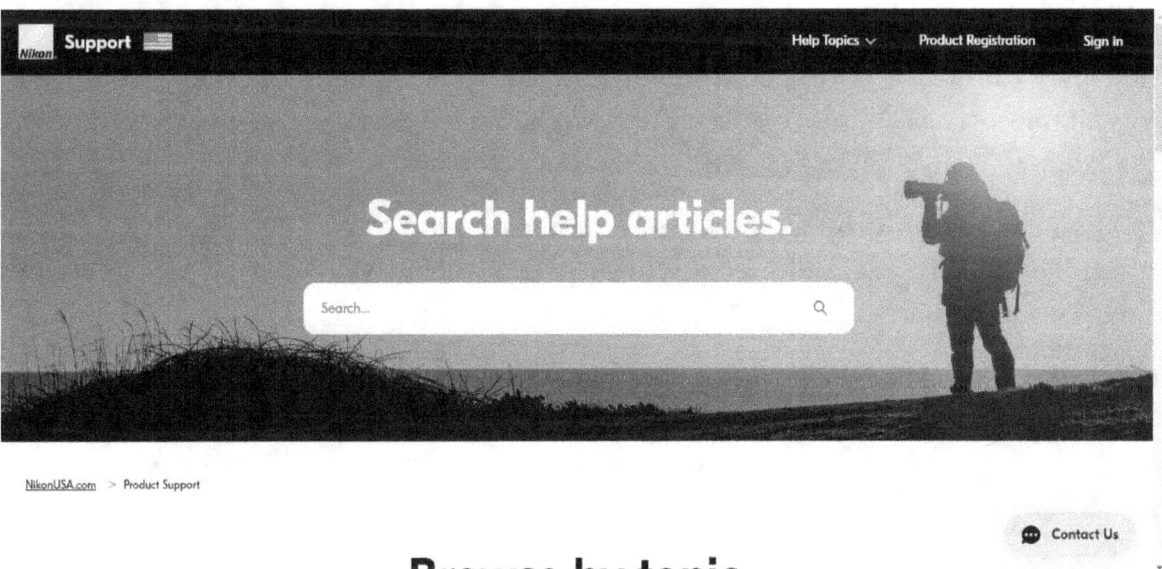

- The website will have a Support section with various resources, including FAQs, troubleshooting guides, downloads (like firmware updates), and contact information.
- You might also find a live chat option available during specific hours.

Phone:

- Nikon offers phone support for various regions. The phone number will be available on the Nikon website's Support section. Here are some examples:

- **USA:** 1-800-NIKON-US (1-800-645-6687) from 9 AM to 8 PM Eastern Time, Monday to Friday.
- **Europe & Africa:** Contact information might vary depending on the specific country. Check the Nikon website for your region.
- **Asia, Oceania & Middle East:** Contact information might vary depending on the specific country. Check the Nikon website for your region.

Email:

- Some Nikon websites offer email support options. Check the specific support page for your region to see if this is available.

Social Media:

- Nikon may have social media channels you can use to reach out with inquiries. However, these might not be the most efficient way for technical support.

Additional Tips:

- **Before contacting support, consult the camera manual or the online resources available on the Nikon website.** You might find the answer to your question without needing to contact them directly.
- **When contacting support, have your camera model (Nikon Coolpix P950) and serial number readily available.** This will help them identify your specific camera and any relevant information.

Be clear and concise about your issue. The more details you provide, the better they can assist you.

THANK YOU FOR READING

www.ingramcontent.com/pod-product-compliance
Lightning Source LLC
Chambersburg PA
CBHW082214220526
45470CB00010B/3158